Drama Wor

Edited by Dan Garr

Scapegoats

Oi You Kids!
Tony Runham

Don't Be a Durr
Michael Maynard

The Pendle Witches
Ann Lister

Scapegoat
Michael Maynard

Published by arrangement
with BBC School Radio

M
MACMILLAN

First published 1984
Reprinted 1985 (twice)

Published by
MACMILLAN EDUCATION LTD
Houndmills, Basingstoke, Hampshire RG21 2XS
and London
Companies and representatives
throughout the world

Printed in Hong Kong

British Library Cataloguing in Publication Data
Runham, Tony
Scapegoats.—(Drama workshop plays)
1. Children's plays, English 2. English
drama—20th century
I. Title II. Maynard, Michael
III. Lister, Ann IV. Garrett, Dan
V. Series
822'.914'08 PR1272
ISBN 0–333–36055–9

Preface

Drama Workshop Plays are intended for 11 to 13 year-olds to read or to act in class or in groups. They have been adapted from scripts originally written for the BBC radio series *Drama Workshop*. As broadcast, the scripts were deliberately incomplete, to act as springboards for classroom drama. In these versions, new scenes have been written, and the plays are complete in themselves.

Each volume contains four plays grouped under a broad thematic heading. The plays have been chosen for their variety in content and style, and for their suitability in different kinds of classroom or drama club use. Some are realistic and down-to-earth, others are historically based, or are ventures into some kind of (often ugly) future. The first play in each volume is usually closest to the everyday drama of young people's own lives; the plays that follow become progressively more demanding.

Some of the plays have large enough casts for most young people in a class to have a different part. Others are more suited to group work, but a whole class can easily be involved if different groups work on different scenes. The play can then be read or performed with each group doing its scene in succession.

For English work, teachers will find *Drama Workshop Plays* suitable for reading and for discussion, and to spark off playwriting. For drama, teachers will find them a useful introduction to scripted work since they allow plenty of scope for improvisation, and they have a free-flowing form close to the idiom of young people's own drama. The more ambitious may wish to rehearse the plays and perform them in a workshop setting, or record them as radio or video plays. Most of the plays make a point about some social or moral issue which can stimulate a variety of follow-up work. For this reason teachers will also find them valuable for RE. Full notes on using the plays are at the back of each volume.

Acknowledgement

The author and publishers are grateful to Lancashire Libraries Department, Lancashire County Council, for permission to reproduce extracts from *The Pendle Witches* by Walter Bennett, 1957.

Contents

About the writers

Tony Runham is a drama teacher and lecturer who is now head of a London school. He has been writing *Drama Workshop* scripts for several years.

Michael Maynard is an actor with many theatre and television credits, and a writer who has devised pieces for many Theatre-in-Education teams, especially Greenwich Young People's Theatre, and Theatre Centre. He has written for *Drama Workshop* for the past seven years.

Ann Lister was a founder member of the Belgrade Theatre-in-Education team at Coventry, and has wide drama teaching experience. She is a regular *Drama Workshop* contributor.

Dan Garrett started work in the theatre, has had wide drama teaching and lecturing experience, and is currently a Senior Drama Producer with BBC School Radio.

Introduction

The plays in this volume are all about *scapegoats*.

All of us from time to time try to lay the blame on somebody else for the things that have gone wrong with our lives. Sometimes we may be justified. After all, if someone snatches our purse or our wallet, it really is because of them that we can't buy the things we set out to get. There are other occasions, though, when we may not want to face up to the fact that the fault lies in ourselves. We may then accuse someone else of making things go wrong for us, perhaps because we don't like them, or because we think they are different from ourselves, or perhaps because they seem to us to act strangely. But if we accuse them without a shred of evidence, then really, we're making *scapegoats* of them. That's what this volume is about – people who are blamed, quite unfairly, for others' misfortunes.

Oi You Kids!

by Tony Runham

Cast: **Danny**
Jane, his sister
Steve, his brother
Danny's mum
Mr Steadman
Mr Steadman's cleaner, Mrs Bryant

1 *A suburban street with large old houses. Danny and his younger brother and sister, Steve and Jane, are playing football.*

Danny: Come on, Steve, pass.

Jane: Over here.

Steve: Oi, foul.

Danny: Never.

Jane: Go on, shoot.

(Danny kicks the ball into a garden and it hits the front door)

Danny: Oh no. It's in old Steadman's garden. Nip in and get it quick, Steve.

Steve: You must be joking. He'll kill me. It's your ball, Danny. You get it.

Danny: He won't mind you. It's me he's got it in for. *(Pause)* You get it, Jane.

Jane: It'll be all right if you're not rude.

(The door opens and Mr Steadman comes out. He picks up the ball.)

Danny: Told you so.

Mr Steadman: You children. Come here.

Jane: *(Quietly)* Who's he calling children?

Mr S: Come here I said.

Steve: Evening, Mr Steadman. Sorry about that.

Mr S: Is this your ball?

Danny: *(Fairly quietly)* Well, it's not a boomerang.

Jane: Shut up, Danny. Sorry, Mr Steadman. Can we have it back, please?

Mr S: What's it doing in my garden?

Danny: Planting geraniums.

Mr S: I heard that.

Steve: Oh shut up, Danny.

Danny: *(Less politely than Jane)* Can we have our ball back? I'm one goal down.

Mr S: You've no right to be playing in the street like that. I've told you before. It's not a football pitch, it's a public thoroughfare. Disturbing people with rowdy games.

Jane: Sorry, Mr Steadman. We'll go down the road a bit. All right? Can we have our ball back now?

Mr S: What's a young girl like you doing anyway, playing football in the street? It's bad enough with hooligans like your brother . . .

Danny: Who's a hooligan?

Mr S: . . . but when girls are out until all hours I don't know what things are coming to.

Jane: Mum doesn't mind.

Mr S: Well she should. This used to be a respectable street.

Danny: Here we go again. Give us our ball back, then we'll go down the road so we don't disturb you any more.

Mr S: You've no right to play football anywhere in this street.

Danny: What's it got to do with you? You don't own it.

Mr S: You'd better mind your manners, young man.

Danny: It's none of your business where we play. Give us our ball back.

Mr S: Don't you talk to me like that.

Danny: That's our ball. Give it back.

Mr S: And it's my garden. You should have thought of that before you kicked your ball over my fence.

(Mr Steadman goes towards his door as Mrs Bryant, his cleaner, comes out)

Mrs Bryant: I've finished upstairs, and I've left your lunch on the table, so I'll be off . . . You all right? You look quite upset.

Mr S: It's those children again. Playing ball in the street. No respect for people's property.

Mrs B: They're only young. I'm sure they don't mean any harm.

Mr S: They just don't seem to know how to behave.

Mrs B: You were young once, Mr S.

Danny: *(Trying to attract Mr Steadman's attention)* Hey!

Mr S: *(Deliberately ignoring him)* I didn't carry on like they do now. We knew how to behave ourselves.

Mrs B: You shouldn't get yourself all worked up.

Mr S: It's changed since the war. All flats now. Cars parked everywhere. And children . . .

Mrs B: They've got to play somewhere. *(She tries to get past him)* Anyway, I must be . . .

Jane: Hey, mister . . .

Mr S: We didn't play in the street. We played in our gardens. And we treated our elders with respect. That Danny, he's the worst of the lot. Just look at him. *(Behind his back, Danny is making an elaborate performance of being bored)* You know, this football of his spends more time in my garden than anywhere else. I don't know. My boys didn't behave like that.

Mrs B: I'm sure they didn't. Anyway, I must be off. I'll be back the same time tomorrow. *(She goes off. Mr Steadman goes in through his door, still holding the football.)*

Steve: Oi, that's our ball.

Jane: Blooming cheek.

Danny: *(Shouting)* Give it back, you old misery.

Steve: Leave it out, Danny, there's no point.

Danny: He can't just take our ball and walk off.

Steve: He just has.

Danny: Yeah, and won't he be sorry. Fancy a game of knock-down-ginger?

Steve: Come off it, Danny. You try knocking on his door and running away and he'll kill you.

Danny: He'll have to catch me first. He's got a bad leg.

Steve: It's not worth it. It won't make him give us the ball back.

Danny: You're chicken.

Steve: No I'm not. It's just stupid.

Jane: I'll do it.

Danny: Don't tell me you're turning into a juvenile delinquent!

Jane: I'm sick of him and his 'respectable street'. Come on, Steve, it's only a game.

Steve: You can do what you like. I'm going to see if I can borrow a ball from somewhere. *(He goes off)*

Danny: What's the matter with him? Come on then, Janey. Who's first?

Jane: Me. You hide over there. With his leg he'll never come that far.

(Danny hides on one side of the stage. Jane goes to Mr Steadman's door, knocks loudly on it, and runs to hide with Danny. The door opens and Mr Steadman comes out. He looks around.)

Mr S: Who's there? Who is it? *(He looks around again and goes in)*

Danny: My turn now.

(He runs across, knocks, and runs back. Mr Steadman comes out again, rather annoyed.)

Mr S: Who's there? I know someone's out here.

(Danny and Jane burst out laughing. Mr Steadman still can't see them.)

Mr S: Any more of this and I'll call the police.

(Danny imitates a police siren. Mr Steadman gets increasingly angry.)

Mr S: I know you're there. *(He clearly cannot see where they are hiding)*

Danny: *(Imitating a parrot)* Who's a naughty boy, then, who's a naughty boy?

Mr S: It's you, Daniel Johnson, isn't it? I shall be round to see your mother.

Danny: *(Mimicking him)* Daniel Johnson. Ooh, Daniel Johnson. Naughty Daniel. Tut, tut, tut.

Mr S: You haven't heard the last of this. *(He slams the door)*

(Danny and Jane stand up and walk towards his house. They are laughing.)

Jane: Come on, that's enough. He'll be waiting by the door now.

Danny: Just once more.

Jane: He'll catch you.

Danny: No he won't. I'm going to ring his bell with this stone. *(He bends down and picks up a stone)*

Jane: You're mad. You'll break something.

Danny: Want to bet. *(He throws the stone. Sounds of breaking glass off stage.)*

Danny: Scarper! *(They both run off)*

2 *Mr Steadman's front hall. There is a knock on the door and Mr Steadman comes on and opens it. Mrs Johnson, Danny's mother, comes in.*

Mr S: Mrs Johnson? I hardly expected to see you here.

Mrs J: Danny told me what happened.

Mr S: He did? I'm surprised.

Mrs J: I'm ever so sorry, Mr Steadman. Honestly, I just don't know what to do with them sometimes.

Mr S: It would be more appropriate if your son came and apologised.

Mrs J: I know, and he probably will in the end. He's stupid sometimes, but he really didn't mean to break your window. He was trying to ring your bell with a stone.

Mr S: He told you that?

Mrs J: Janey said the same thing. They don't lie to me, Mr Steadman.

Mr S: That's as may be, but it doesn't alter the fact that I have a broken window. And apart from that, I'm too old to be troubled by children playing knock-down-ginger.

Mrs J: They didn't say anything about that.

Mr S: I don't suppose they did.

Mrs J: I don't know what to say. They make me so mad sometimes.

Mr S: I was really angry myself earlier, I don't mind telling you. Then I remembered something. My dad once gave me a good hiding for doing the same thing. . . . I think I may have been a bit touchy lately. I must be getting old. And this leg of mine doesn't get any better.

Mrs J: Have you seen the doctor?

Mr S: They haven't found any cure for old age. . . . Your husband's not at home any more, is he?

Mrs J: He left a year ago. Danny's been pretty wild since then.

Mr S: *(Drily)* I had noticed . . . I'd like to sort this out, you know. I'm too old for street fighting. If you could encourage them to play further down the road . . .

Mrs J: Oh, I will. And Danny will pay for the window.

Mr S: Do you think he would bring the money round himself? Perhaps if we were to talk a little more calmly . . .

Mrs J: I'll try and get him to come round after tea. I'm really ever so grateful.

Mr S: I don't want any more unpleasantness. And I can do without any more broken windows.

3 *The kitchen in Danny's house. Danny, Jane, Steve and Mrs Johnson are sitting round the kitchen table having tea.*

Danny: I suppose he told you I should be locked up.

Mrs J: Serve you right too. You're really stupid sometimes.

Jane: It wasn't just Danny. It was all of us.

Steve: Not me, it wasn't. I was trying to borrow a football.

Danny: No, it wasn't anything to do with Steve.

Mrs J: Oh, shut up the lot of you. Honestly, Janey, I thought you had more sense.

Jane: Well . . .

Danny: What's it got to do with him if we play in the street?

Mrs J: A lot if you break his windows.

Danny: I didn't mean to.

Mrs J: You should know better at your age.

Danny: Is he going to get me into trouble?

Mrs J: You've done that yourself. Banging on people's doors and breaking their windows.

Danny: Well, he shouldn't have taken our football.

Mrs J: No, and that's what he said too.

Steve: Get away.

Jane: He said that?

Danny: I don't believe you.

Mrs J: You listen to me. He's not so bad. He thinks some of it's his own fault.

Danny: Why does he keep going on at us then?

Mrs J: Probably because you deserve it. He's not well, you know. He lives there on his own, he's got a bad leg, and he's not a young man. Are you surprised he gets sick of people disturbing him and breaking his windows? Honestly, Danny . . .

Danny: Well . . .

Mrs J: Don't you 'Well' me. He could have made a right fuss. But he wants to get things sorted out.

Danny: What have I got to do?

Mrs J: You'll have to pay for the window . . .

Danny: Great.

Mrs J: . . . and you'll have to go round there and apologise. You can get that over when you've finished the tea.

Danny: I can't.

Mrs J: Oh yes you can. Please, Danny. I can't cope with any more of this.

Danny: Oh, all right. Steve, did you borrow another ball?

Steve: Why? You want to kick that through his window now?

Danny: I thought we'd have a game after. Down the other end.

Steve: It's by the door.

Mrs J: Oh, go on, Danny. Get on with it.

Danny: All right, I'm going. What a life.

4 *The street. Danny comes on dribbling the ball and kicking it against the fence.*

Danny: And Johnson takes it in mid-field, moves quickly across, and . . . yes . . . he beats him . . . I think he might score . . . he shoots . . .

(He mis-kicks the ball, and once again it goes into Mr Steadman's garden. Again there is the sound of breaking glass.)

Danny: Oh no!

(Mr Steadman opens his door furiously)

Mr S: You again. I should have known . . .

Danny: Honest, Mr Steadman, it was an accident. I didn't mean to . . .

Mr S: You didn't mean to. . . . You didn't mean to . . .

Danny: *(Quietly)* I'm sorry, Mr Steadman. Really I am. I'll pay for the window.

Mr S: You will indeed. Wait there. I'm calling the police.

Danny: There's no need for that. It was an accident.

Mr S: Accident! You have the nerve to tell me that, after you've been making my life a misery for days. Well you've gone too far this time. Just you wait there.

Danny: Like hell I will . . . *(Danny runs off)*

Mr S: Come back here at once. You can't just run away from this . . . *(He stomps back into his house.)*

5 *The back garden of an empty house. There is an old shed there in which Danny is hiding. Jane and Steve climb in over the fence.*

Jane: Danny, are you there?

Steve: Come on, where are you? The Flying Squad and Interpol are combing the country for you.

(Danny comes out of the shed)

Danny: Ha ha. Very funny. Have you got anything to eat? I'm starving.

Jane: Here. *(She gives him a sandwich)*

Danny: Cheese. Great. *(He starts to eat hungrily)* Have you told anyone where I am?

Jane: Course not. Anyway, we didn't actually know you were here.

Steve: So when the copper asked if we knew where you are we said no. I mean, we didn't really. We just guessed.

Danny: What copper?

Jane: Mr Steadman told the police.

Steve: He said you'd been . . . er . . . harry something or other.

Jane: Harassing him. Picking on him.

Danny: Blimey. What did Mum say?

Steve: She's furious. She'll kill you – if Steadman doesn't.

Jane: He's going to have you taken to court.

Danny: He's never. Not over a couple of windows.

Jane: He is, Danny. Wilful damage to property, the copper said.

Danny: But it wasn't my fault. I was on my way to apologise. It was an accident.

Jane: Mum told them that, but you try making old Steadman believe it.

Danny: Well, she wouldn't lie about it, would she?

Steve: You aren't half in trouble, Danny. What are you going to do?

Danny: Dunno . . . *(He thinks for a bit)* I think I'll go round and see old Steadman.

Jane: No point. He won't listen to you.

Danny: I don't suppose he will. He won't even see me.

Steve: What do you mean?

Danny: Simple. If I'm in this much trouble over a broken window . . .

Jane: Two broken windows.

Danny: All right, but they were accidents . . . But if he thinks that's harassment I'll really show him. You see. He's got no right to call Mum a liar.

Jane: He didn't really say that.

Danny: That's what you said. Here! Has he still got those stupid gnomes round the back of his house?

Steve: What?

Danny: You know. Those gnomes in his garden.

Steve: I think so. Why?

Danny: I'm going to have a bit of fun with them, that's why.

Jane: You're mad, Danny. Aren't you in enough trouble?

Danny: Don't worry. I'm not going to harm anything. Just give the old man something to think about. You know. Cheer him up a bit.

Steve: Good idea. Serve him right. Here, Danny, I'll come too.

Jane: Leave it. It's too risky. Let's go home.

Danny: It's all right. You don't have to come.

Jane: Oh shut up. You're too stupid to be trusted on your own.

Danny: Come on then. Just for a laugh. Give him something to remember me by.

Jane: Honest, Danny – just for a laugh?

Danny: Honest. Come on. *(They go off)*

6 *In the street. Danny, Steve and Jane come on quietly.*

Danny: Right. I'll sneak round and see if the coast's clear. Then we'll rearrange his garden for him. If anyone comes, whistle.

(Danny goes off in the direction of Steadman's house. The others wait, watching up and down the road, and becoming increasingly anxious.)

Steve: I'd like to see old Steadman's face when he finds out.

Jane: Yeah, but I don't fancy Mum knowing.

Steve: She won't find out.

Jane: Use your head. He'll know it's us.

Steve: He won't be able to prove it.

Jane: He won't have to if he catches Danny.

Steve: He won't.

Jane: I hope not.

Steve: Me too. All Danny needs now is to be done for breaking and entering.

Jane: Trepass. If it's only the garden it's trespass.

Steve: You sure?

Jane: I think so.

(There is a pause)

Jane: Look out.

(Danny hurries in)

Jane: Is it all right?

Danny. No. No it's not.

Steve: God. Did he see you?

Danny: I don't know.

Steve: You must.

Danny: I don't know if he saw me. He was just lying on the floor groaning.

Jane: Old Steadman?

Danny: Who do you think?

Steve: Where?

Danny: On the floor in the kitchen.

Jane: What were you doing in there?

Danny: I went in, didn't I? The door was open so I just went in. And he was lying on the floor groaning.

Steve: They'll say it was your fault.

Danny: No one saw me.

Jane: But you'll have to tell someone.

Danny: How can I? They'll say I broke into his house.

Steve: You did.

Jane: We can't just leave him there. He might die. We can't, Danny.

Danny: Well what *can* we do?

Steve: Phone an ambulance. Don't give our names.

Danny: 'Excuse me, Mr Ambulance Man, but I've just broken into this house . . .' They wouldn't believe you.

Jane: You could tell Mum.

Danny: Don't be stupid. If she finds out she'll kill me.

Jane: He might die in there.

Danny: I know. All right. I know.

Jane: Well . . .

Danny: I've broken into his house. If the police find out . . .

Steve: Come on, Danny, we've got to do something. It's not just you.

Jane: We've got to, Danny.

Danny: I know. *(He comes to a decision)* Go and tell Mum what's happened. She'll phone an ambulance.

Jane: What about you? You can't run off again.

Danny: S'all right. I'll go back in and wait with him till they get here. Go on. Hurry!

7 *Mr Steadman's front hall. There is a knock on the door and Mr Steadman comes in to answer it. He has a bandage round his head. He opens the door, and Danny, Jane and Steve are on the doorstep.*

Mr S: Oh. I think you'd better come in. *(They do so, and stand about uneasily)* Your mother told me at the hospital what happened.

Danny: I can explain . . .

Mr S: You've told me that before.

Danny: Yes, but . . .

Mr S: Look – I don't know what you were doing in my kitchen, Daniel Johnson, and I don't think I want to. But I'm very glad you were there. It could have been serious for me if you hadn't found me when you did.

Jane: Are you all right now?

Mr S: Yes. Yes thank you.

Steve: What happened?

Mr S: Apparently I had a dizzy spell. Fell over and hit my head.

Danny: You do know why I was in your kitchen, don't you? Mum told you.

Mr S: Yes, I do know.

Danny: I didn't mean to break your windows. Honestly.

Mr S: Hm . . .

Jane: It's the truth, Mr Steadman. Really.

Mr S: All right. I'll believe you.

Danny: I'll pay for them as soon as I can.

Mr S: Thank you, but that won't be necessary. *(There is a pause. The kids look at Mr Steadman, and he clears his throat.)* You have been rather impetuous . . .

Steve: Mum says he never thinks.

Mr S: Yes. She may have a point. But perhaps I have been rather hasty too. And I do appear to owe you a substantial favour.

Danny: Are you sure?

Mr S: I really think it's time we declared a truce. Wait there, please.

(He goes out of the room)

Danny: I don't believe it. He's human after all.

Jane: *(Kicking him)* Shut it, Danny.

(Mr Steadman comes back in. He is carrying a football.)

Mr S: I think this is yours. *(He hands it to Danny)*

Danny: Thanks, Mr Steadman. Thanks a lot.

Mr S: Perhaps you could play with it a little further down the street.

Danny: Don't worry. We will. It's time we broke someone else's windows.

(Blackout/curtain)

'Don't Be a Durr'

by Michael Maynard

Cast: **Gary Barnes**
Marilyn
Zoe
Miss Norton
Dad
Mum
Stuart
Classmates (including Pongo)
Bus Conductor
Passengers

The play is set in the East End of London but it could be adapted to other local areas. The dialect as it stands is 'Cockney'.

1 *A bus. Gary is sitting furthest away from where people get on. Passengers are chatting as they jolt along. It is morning. The bus stops. Marilyn and Zoe push forward laughing and squealing.*

Marilyn: Come on! Mind out! Wait for us!

Zoe: Hang on!

Conductor: Hurry along now please.

(They leap on, out of breath)

Zoe: Beat ya!

Marilyn: Made it.

(The conductor rings the bell and the bus sets off. At various times during the scene the bus stops and starts again.)

Marilyn: Come on!

Zoe: 'Ere Mow [*short for 'Marilyn', rhymes with 'how'*], there's Gary.

Marilyn: Let's go and sit behind him.

Zoe: *(Clomping off)* Yeah, be a laugh.

Marilyn: Sshh!

Zoe: Oh all right.

(They tip-toe up to him)

Zoe: Boo!

Gary: What?! . . . Oh.

Marilyn: Watcha. 'Ow you today?

Gary: H . . . hallo.

Marilyn: Mornin', Durrbrain.

Gary: My name's G . . . Gary.

Marilyn: All right, G . . . G . . . G . . . Gary.

(Marilyn and Zoe snigger. Then, sticking her index finger out, Marilyn taps Gary on the shoulder.)

Marilyn: Eh Gary?

Gary: What?

(He turns around and gets Marilyn's finger on his cheek)

Gary: Ow!

Marilyn: Caught ya.

Gary: Stop p . . . picking on me.

Marilyn: Ugh. Say it, don't spray it.

Zoe: Yeah, say it, don't spray it.

(They giggle)

Marilyn: 'Ere Gary, what's green and hairy, got six legs and a long tail?

Gary: I dunno.

Marilyn: Nor do I *(Running her hand up his back)*, but there's one crawlin' up your back!

Gary: Get off.

Conductor: *(Working his way towards them – collecting fares en route)* Fares please. Any more fares please.

Marilyn: Look at the state of you, Gary Durrbrain Barnes. I mean, Zoe 'ere's a physical mess, but you . . .

Zoe: I'm not! Not like 'im.

Marilyn: . . . but you are an insult to the human race. Look at your cap. *(Ruffling it)* Nick nick nick . . . !

Gary: Leave m . . . me alone, Mow.

Marilyn: Marilyn to you, Durrbrain. (*Pause*) Go on, do your Gonzo.

Gary: No.

Zoe: Yeah, go on, your Gonzo impression.

Gary: N . . . no.

Marilyn: Do it. Do it. *(She prods him rhythmically – Zoe joins in)*

Gary: Stop p . . . p . . . D . . . don't do that.

Marilyn: D . . . durr . . . durr . . . *(She is, by now, into a familiar send-up routine)* One and one are . . . durr!

Zoe: *(Joining in)* Durr. Durr.

Marilyn: Hey, 'ow d'you confuse a durrbrain?

Zoe: How?

Marilyn: Put 'im in a round room and tell 'im to stand in the corner! Get it? Hey, 'nother one. D'you hear about the durrbrain who shot an arrow into the sky . . . and missed! *(They both laugh)*

Conductor: Fares please.

Marilyn: 'Ere. Durrbrain's Mastermind. Question – How d'you pay your fare on a bus? . . . I've started so I'll finish . . . You use your bus . . . what?

Zoe: Pass.

Marilyn: Right. Bus pass. Gettit?

Zoe: Oh.

Conductor: Come on now.

Marilyn: Well, show 'im then. *(They show their passes)*

Conductor: Right. Thanks. Any more fares please.

Marilyn: 'Ow's it feel to be the stupidest person in the world, Gary? I mean, no one's as stupid as you. I mean, Zoe 'ere's a bit durr, but . . .

Zoe: I'm not.

Marilyn: . . . but at least she's good at disco an' that. It's a wonder your Mum and Dad didn't do away wiv you when you was born.

Zoe: Yeah, what you good at?

Gary: I'm g . . . good . . .

Marilyn: I tell you what you're good for.

Zoe: What?

Marilyn: Nuffin'. Good for nuffin'! Gettit?

(Marilyn and Zoe laugh. Gary gets up to go.)

Marilyn: 'Ere, where you off to, Durrbrain?

Zoe: Runnin' away?

Marilyn: Can't take it, eh?

Both: Can't take it.

Gary: It's not that.

Marilyn: What then, Durrbrain?

Zoe: Yeah, what then, Durrbrain?

Gary: It . . . It's time to get off, that's all.

Marilyn: What?

Zoe: *(Realising)* Oh yeah . . . it's our stop.

Marilyn: Oh no! Nearly missed it. *(They rush off)* That was your fault, Durrbrain.

2 *The classroom of a boisterous school. The class includes Gary, Marilyn, Zoe and Pongo. There is lots of noise and activity.*

Miss Norton: Quieten down now. Come on 2J. Quieten down. Now then, I'm Miss Norton and I'll be taking you while Mr Jones is on leave. Obviously it'll take me a while to get to know you all, but I'm sure I will in time. Right, before next period I'm going to ask you a few questions. *(A few 'Oh no's' from the class)* By the way, who's the register monitor?

Marilyn: Go on Pongo . . . that's you.

Pongo: Don't call me that.

Marilyn: Pongo, Pongo. *(General laughter)*

Miss Norton: Quiet. What's your name?

Pongo: Steven White, Sir . . . I mean Miss. *(General laughter)*

Marilyn: But he's really Pongo, Miss. 'Cos 'e pongs! *(Laughter)*

Miss Norton: Quiet! Right Steven, take the register to the office now.

Marilyn: *(Under breath)* Pongo. *(General suppressed sniggers)*

Miss Norton: Now then, who can tell me what's special about today? What happens today that makes this date famous?

Marilyn: *(Putting her hand up)* I know, Miss.

Miss Norton: It's . . . Marilyn, isn't it?

Marilyn: Marilyn Hicks, yes Miss.

Miss Norton: Well, tell me.

Marilyn: It's Gary, Miss. It's the day he goes to the mind-reader.

Miss Norton: *(Bewildered)* Pardon?

Marilyn: It's the day Gary goes to the mind-reader. But they only charge 'im half-price. Gettit? *(Laughter and sniggers)*

Miss Norton: Look, I've no idea what you're talking about . . .

Marilyn: Him . . . Gary. That's what.

Miss Norton: Gary? Yes well, perhaps Gary can answer my question. What's special about . . .

Marilyn: Oh no Miss.

Miss Norton: What?

Marilyn: Don't ask Gary, please.

Miss Norton: Why on earth not?

Marilyn: Well, you know, he's a bit . . . durr! *(Laughter)* If you ask 'im we'll never get home this week.

Miss Norton: I shan't tell you again, Marilyn. Be quiet and give someone else a chance to speak. Now then Gary, do you know what's significant about today's date?

Gary: Yes miss, it's err . . . err . . .

Marilyn: *(Imitating)* Durr . . . durr . . . (*Laughter*)

Miss Norton: Quiet!

Gary: It's err . . .

Marilyn: Come on, we'll miss games at this rate.

Miss Norton: That's enough, Marilyn. Just leave him alone.

Marilyn: But Miss, 'e's only good at one thing . . .

Zoe: Yeah, everyone knows that.

Miss Norton: *(Irritated but patient)* Oh yes, and what's that?

Marilyn: His Gonzo impression. *[Or any other impression that the actor playing Gary can do]*

Zoe: Yeah, go on Durr, show Miss. Do it.

Miss Norton: What is it, Gary?

Gary: It's on the err . . . Mmm . . .

Zoe: Y'know Miss, the loony one on the Muppets.

Marilyn: The ugly one.

Zoe: 'E's great at that. Looks just like 'im.

Marilyn: Go on Durr, do it, do it.

(Gary does it. The class laughs.)

Miss Norton: Right, that's it! That's quite enough. Silence! I can see I'm going to get little sense out of you lot today. However, I can . . .

(Pips over tannoy – or other end-of-lesson signal. They get up to rush out.)

Miss Norton: Sit down! Stay where you are! *(They do so)* I can assure you we will finish this conversation at the end of school today. *(General 'Oh, no's')* And you won't be going home until some sense is spoken. Now . . . off to your next lesson. *(They get up and go)* Oh Gary, come here a moment please.

Zoe: *(As she leaves)* Go on, Durrbrain. *(To Marilyn)* I reckon she fancies 'im. *(Miss Norton and Gary are left alone)*

Miss Norton: Now then Gary, what's all this about?

Gary: What Miss?

Miss Norton: Why do they taunt you like this?

Gary: I d . . . dunno Miss.

Miss Norton: Listen, it's one thing to have a stutter – I'm sure something can be done about that – but why do you let them make fun of you?

Gary: Err . . .

Miss Norton: All this playing the fool for them. It only makes it worse, you know.

Gary: It makes them laugh. 'Least they don't . . . you know.

Miss Norton: You think it's a way of being . . . *(Tries for the correct word)* . . . accepted? Is that it?

Gary: 'Spose so.

Miss Norton: But it only makes things worse for you in the long run. Can't you see that? Oh look, you'd better go, or you'll be late. I'll talk to you later.

3 *Gary's home. The kitchen/diner. Mum is busy clearing things away.*

Dad: *(Coming in from outside)* Hello love. Is 'e 'ere yet?

Mum: No, not yet.

Dad: Gaw, I'm starving. Give 's a bit of bread and cheese while we wait.

Mum: Not now dear, you'll spoil your tea.

Dad: When've I ever spoilt me tea, eh?

Mum: Well, get it yourself. I'm busy.

(She clears some more things away. moving Dad out of the way in order to get to cupboards and things. Dad grumbles and gets some food.)

Dad: It's only the new lodger coming round; it ain't Prince Charles, y'know.

Mum: I wanna make a good impression. I don't want 'im thinking the place is a dump.

Dad: Come off it, 'e's only a student. Probably lives in a pig sty.

Mum: No, 'e sounded very nice on the phone.

Dad: Oh yeah? Well-spoken, was 'e? All we need – some toffee-nosed smarty-pants intellectual around the 'ouse.

(Gary comes home from school)

Gary: H . . . Hello, Mum.

Mum: 'Allo love. Wipe your feet.

Gary: Hello D . . . dad.

Dad: Gary.

Gary: Oh crisps . . . great. What f . . . flavour?

Dad: Getcha 'ands off. You'll spoil your tea. Besides, we got the new lodger coming in a minute.

Gary: Who's that?

Mum: He's a student. He'll be staying with us. Well, since your Nan . . . you know . . . *(meaning died)* . . . we've got the room free, so . . .

Dad: So don't you go bothering 'im.

Gary: Who is 'e?

Mum: From the local tech.

Gary: I wonder if . . .

Dad: Look, just keep your mouth shut. We don't want 'im knowing there's an idiot in the 'ouse.

Mum: *(Weakly reprimanding)* Colin! You shouldn't say that.

Dad: I wish 'e'd 'urry up, whoever 'e is. I'm famished.

(The door bell rings)

Mum: That'll be 'im now.

Gary: Shall I answer . . .

Dad: No, I'd better get it.

(He goes to the door and opens it)

Stuart: Mr Barnes?

Dad: Yeah.

Stuart: I'm Stuart Andrews.

Dad: *(Bringing him through to the kitchen/diner)* Come in. Come on in, son. This 'ere's Stuart. That's Gary . . .

Stuart: Hi.

Dad: And my wife . . . uh . . . Mrs Barnes.

Stuart: Hello.

Mum: Hello. Yes, we spoke on the phone.

Dad: Come on then. Betcha must be hungry, eh?

Stuart: Well, not exactly . . .

Dad: Thought you must be. Right. Dish up, Ma. Come on, son, y'can sort your stuff out later. Sit yerself down.

Stuart: Oh thanks.

(All except Mum sit down at the dining table)

Dad: Now then . . . student, are ya?

Stuart: Yes.

Dad: Watcha studying then?

Stuart: Well, sociology.

Dad: *(Ignorantly)* Oh yeah. Be a social worker like?

Stuart: Not exactly.

Gary: What does s . . . sociology mean?

Dad: Don't mind 'im, Stuart. He's just a bit *(Whispers)* . . . y'know.

Mum: 'Ere we are then. Now 'elp yourselves.

Dad: *(Already eating)* Yeah, get stuck in, son. Go on.

Stuart: Oh great, thanks . . .

Gary: Would you l . . . like . . .

Dad: *(Grabbing the plate)* Get yer 'ands off, Gary. Let the guests eat first.

Gary: B . . . but I was only p . . . passing it . . .

Dad: Eat, Gary. Just shut up and eat. Let's all eat. 'Nuff talkin' for now.

(They all eat)

4 *The dining table. Fifteen minutes later. Just finishing eating.*

Dad: Anyone want this last bit of 'am?

Stuart: I've had plenty, thanks.

Gary: I w . . . wouldn't m . . . mind . . .

Dad: No one? Well, can't let it go to waste. *(He stuffs it down. Pause as they all sit back.)*

Dad: Well, off out now then, are you son?

Stuart: No, I don't go out much actually.

Dad: Well what d'you do with your time? What are your hobbies?

Stuart: I'm more interested in reading and . . . uh, well, playing chess and things. I don't suppose anyone fancies a game do they?

Dad: What . . . of chess?

Stuart: Yes. Do you . . . ?

Dad: Don't know 'ow, son. Darts is my game.

Stuart: What about you, Gary, do you play?

Gary: N . . . no.

Stuart: Don't fancy learning, do you?

Dad: Don' think 'e'd be able. Not very bright, y'see.

Stuart: Oh, it's easier than you think. What do you reckon, Gary?

Gary: Yeah.

Stuart: Great. Now help me get the board set up.

(He gets the board and the chess set and starts setting them up)

Gary: It's a draughts board.

Stuart: That's right, it's the same thing.

Dad: Wasting your time. 'E'll never learn.

Stuart: *(Not bothering to discuss it)* There, now these are the pieces. You take all the white ones and we'll sort them out. Now these are the pawns. Right, line them up. This is the rook.

Gary: What, the castle thing?

Stuart: Yeah, it's sometimes called a castle. You should have two of them.

Gary: I've got them.

Stuart: Now, the bishops . . . here. And the knights should . . .

Gary: What, the horsey ones?

Stuart: That's it. There . . . and there. Oh by the way, I'll play with you, but only on one condition.

Gary: What's that?

Stuart: Once you've learnt, and got good . . . you have to let me win occasionally!

(They both laugh and get ready to play)

5 *An ice-cream parlour. The place sells ice-cream and hot-dogs. In a corner it has various video machine games. Gary is playing one of the machines. Taped sound effects could be used, or actors simulating the sounds themselves.*

Marilyn: *(Rushing in)* Come on, Zoe, we've gotta get there before the third years.

Zoe: All right. *(Seeing Gary)* Oh no . . . Gary! How'd he get 'ere first?

Marilyn: What you doing 'ere, Durrbrain?

Gary: I'm playing the machine.

Marilyn: I can see that. I'm not durr like you. But you're gonna have to go now, 'cos the good players have arrived.

Zoe: Hey Mow, 'e's got ever such a high score . . . look!

Marilyn: Oh yeah, not such a durr that he don't know how to cheat, eh?

Gary: I d . . . don't cheat.

Marilyn: Come on then . . . I fancy beating someone. I'll give you a game. Loser buys the ice-creams, right? You put the money in, go on.

Gary: But I've only got one 10p left.

Marilyn: Just right . . . Bung it in then, and *(Doing so)* I'll press the two-player button. *(The machine responds)* I'll go first.

Zoe: But what about me?

Marilyn: You're the judge, ent yer? Keep score, an' that. Here I go. *(Machine sounds)* Yeah. Pow!

(Marilyn makes her own explosive sounds along with the machine. Meanwhile Zoe intersperses with . . .)

Zoe: Player one . . . 50 . . . 75 . . . 100 . . . 140 . . . *(Excited)* There's the monster, the monster . . .

Marilyn: The alien, you idiot, the alien . . .

Zoe: Go on Mow, go on.

Marilyn: Oh!

Zoe: You missed it.

Marilyn: Just shut up and call the score.

Zoe: 600, 650 . . . 690 . . . 740 . . . Oh . . . it's gone.

Marilyn: Stupid machine.

Zoe: 850! Gary's turn now.

Marilyn: Go on Durr . . . your turn.

Zoe: Player two. 50 . . . 90 . . . 150 . . . 190 . . . 270 . . . Cor, in 'e good, Mow? 350 . . . hey, they gotcha.

Gary: I didn't see that one.

Zoe: Go. 410 . . . 500 . . . 550 . . . Wow . . . Here's the monster, the alien thingey. Woww!! He got it. He got it.

Marilyn: Shut up, Zoe, just shut up.

Zoe: 850 . . . 900 . . . 970 . . . 1000. . . . Wow . . . (*The machine stops*) That's it. 1400. That's the highest (*Truly impressed*) 1400!

Gary: I'll have chocolate chip, two scoops please.

Marilyn: You can stick that! I've got too much to do, to play silly games. Come on, Zoe. (*She goes*)

Zoe: (*Following*) Oh but Mow, I ain't 'ad a go yet . . .

6 *Stuart's bedroom. Stuart and Gary are playing chess. Gary plays quickly. Stuart struggles rather.*

Stuart: (*Triumphant, at last*) Now then, I'll move my knight here, thus threatening both your queen . . . and your rook. See.

(*He keeps his finger on the knight, making sure he's made the right move*)

Gary: B . . . but . . .

Stuart: No buts about it, Gary. (*Takes his finger away, smugly confident*) Just get out of that if you can.

Gary: (*Moving bishop*) There . . . Check mate.

Stuart: What?

Gary: I tried to warn you, b . . . but . . .

Stuart: You cunning devil. Sometimes I think you put that stutter on deliberately . . . just so that people will underestimate you.

Gary: I wouldn't d . . . do that.

Stuart: No, you wouldn't, would you.

Gary: N . . . no.

Stuart: I bet it gives you a kick though, eh? Slaughtering me like that?

Gary: N . . . no, not really. I like it when it's a close game and you d . . . don't know till the last minute who's going to win.

Stuart: Me too. But I'm not even coming close these days. I mean, what did I do wrong this time?

Gary: You c . . . castled too early and left your king defenceless.

Stuart: Tch, blast.

Gary: You taught me never to do that.

Stuart: Fool I am . . . You know, you're a very talented player. It's amazing how quickly you've caught on. Hasn't anyone realised how bright you are?

Gary: They think I'm stupid, just 'cos I c . . . can't talk properly.

Stuart: Yes, I can believe that. You know, I think it's about time you played somebody else.

Gary: I only like playing you.

Stuart: Only because you can beat me, I bet!

Gary: N . . . no, it's not that. You know.

Stuart: Yes, well . . . nevertheless, how about a trip up West, on Saturday?

Gary: Why . . . what's . . . ?

Stuart: Well, in a certain chess department of a certain big store, a certain top class Russian chess master is taking on all-comers. And it seems to me that a certain young chess player might like to have a go.

Gary: *(Excited, but . . .)* B . . . but how? I mean . . .

Stuart: They have about eight boards set out and he circulates, playing them all. It's interesting. You don't stand a chance, of course, but it's really good experience. What do you think? Fancy trying your luck?

7 *The Classroom. Miss Norton isn't there. The class chatter. Pongo rushes in thinking he's late.*

Pongo: *(Breathless)* Where's Miss?

Marilyn: S'all right Pongo, she's wiv the Head. Said she'd be a bit late.

Zoe: I wonder what's up.

Marilyn: Prob'ly talking about putting Gary down.

Zoe: What . . . in another class?

Marilyn: No . . . put 'im down . . . like a dog when they're mad, you know.

Zoe: Oh yeah.

Marilyn: You hear that, Durrbrain? You're really gonna cop it this time.

Zoe: Yeah, you've 'ad it this time, Gonzo.

Marilyn: They've realised at last you ain't worth bovvering wiv. I mean, what've you ever done, eh?

Zoe: Good for nuffin', that's 'im.

Marilyn: I mean, Zoe's a bit durr, in't she . . .

Zoe: Get off!

Marilyn: . . . but at least she can run fast . . .

Zoe: Faster'n you, Mow.

Marilyn: I know, I know. But I'm the star of drama, ain't I? I mean, who got all the laughs in the school play the other night?

Zoe: Yeah, you was funny in that, Mow.

Marilyn: Course I was. Talented, you see. Not like old Durrbrain!

Miss Norton: *(Entering)* All right, 2J. Quiet now. Listen. Quiet. Now, I've got a bit of a surprise for you today.

Marilyn: Don't tell me, Gary got a question right!

Miss Norton: Quiet. We're going to have a visit from a reporter and a photographer. *(General 'Wow's' and other expressions of excitement)* The local paper wants to interview you all and take some pictures of the class.

Class: Way hey!!

Zoe: Why, Miss?

Marilyn: What d'ya mean 'why'? Must be 'cos of me and the school play. Is that right, Miss? They want to interview me about how I feel being a star, an' that?

Miss Norton: Oh no. Hasn't anyone told you? It's nothing to do with you, Marilyn. It's Gary. Didn't you know? The Press want to take photographs of him with his schoolfriends.

Zoe: But why?

Marilyn: What's he done? Started talking properly or summink?

Miss Norton: Oh no . . . He played chess against a famous Russian chess player the other day . . . and won. He was the only person to beat the great chess master. They think he could be a tournament player if he wants.

(Assorted 'Wows' and applause. The class crowd round Gary, congratulating him loudly. Marilyn is left with her mouth gaping open, speechless, near Miss Norton.)

Miss Norton: Not such a 'Durrbrain' after all, eh Marilyn?

The Pendle Witches

by Ann Lister

Cast:

Headline
Old Chattox
Anne Redfern } her daughters
Bessie Chattox }
John Bulcock
Jane Bulcock, his mother
Old Mother Demdike
Elizabeth Davies, her daughter
Alizon Davies }
James Davies } children of Elizabeth Davies
Jennet Davies }
Christopher Holgate
Elizabeth Holgate, his wife
Katherine Hewitt
Alice Gray
Richard Baldwin
Ellen Baldwin, his daughter
Priest
John Law, a pedlar
Thomas Potts
Roger Nowell
Judge Bromley
Judge Altham
Agnes Thompson
Knowall Gossip
Inquisitive Gossip
Scared Gossip
Sympathetic Gossip
Gaolers
Guards

1 *Gawthorpe Village Green*

Headline: Lancashire, 1611. Gawthorpe Village Green.

Chattox: Fancy, pretty Fancy! *(Goes on mumbling while gossips look on)*

Inquisitive Gossip: Look at her! Old Chattox.

Scared Gossip: Old witch.

Knowall Gossip: Witch Chattox.

Sympathetic Gossip: She's feeble and poor.

Kn Gossip: And hungry. Going mad with hunger, I shouldn't wonder.

Symp Gossip: Simple-minded, that's all it is.

Kn Gossip: No – she's a witch.

Sc Gossip: Her daughter's a witch.

Inq Gossip: Anne Redfern?

Kn Gossip: Oh yes, Anne Redfern's a witch.

Inq Gossip: She's Chattox's daughter, that's why.

Sc Gossip: And Old Chattox is a witch.

Kn Gossip: Yes, she's an evil witch, Chattox is.

Inq Gossip: Oh, Chattox is, yes.

Sc Gossip: Chattox . . .

Potts: She was a very withered and decrepit creature, her sight almost gone. . . . Her lips ever chattering and talking, but no man knew what.

Headline: Thomas Potts – Clerk to the Judges of the Lancaster Assize.

Potts: Old Chattox – her real name was Anne Whittle – was a wool-carder and belonged to a coven of witches in Pendle Forest. Many witches like her were very poor, disfigured and feeble-minded. Chattox's daughter Anne Redfern was very likely brought up as a witch.

Anne Redfern: We lived in a cottage by a stream in West Close near Pendle Hall. We never had enough to eat . . . my sister Bessie became a nifty thief!

I often saw my mother alone, talking to herself. Sometimes the village people would come to us for herbal remedies when they were ill, but more often than not they would stare and avoid us. I remember being different from other people. Then came the day when I was initiated into the Coven.

2 *Pendle Forest. Chattox, Jane and John Bulcock and Bessie Chattox meet for the Initiation Ceremony.*

Chattox: Prepare the black hen for sacrifice.

John Bulcock: The legs I bind . . . the wings I bind . . . Now . . .

(While the hen is being killed by John Bulcock, the witches scream and clap in ritual)

Chattox: Now, John Bulcock, bind Anne Redfern to the pole.

(Rhythmical feet-stamping while Anne is bound to the pole. Then the witches stamp-dance round the pole in ritual, chanting and clapping. John Bulcock holds the Black Book.)

John Bulcock: Place your hands on the Black Book. Take the oath. Do ye promise to deny the life that ye have lived?

Anne: I do deny it willingly.

John: Do ye swear to pawn your soul to the power of Witchcraft?

Anne: Yes I will, Grand Master.

John: The spirits will assist you in whatever you desire.

Chattox: Prick her finger, John Bulcock. *(Laughing and mumbling)* Now, Anne Redfern, make yer sign in blood on the Infernal Covenant. *(Jane Bulcock holds the Covenant* *for Anne to sign)* And in the Black Book. *(John Bulcock offers the book for Anne to sign)*

Witches: *(Chanting)* Spirits come and give her power. Come and give her power. Spirits come – give her power – power!

Anne: Give me power. Give me power. Give me power! *(She breaks from the pole in triumph)*

John: Now ye have power by the assistance of the imps. They will send you to do what mischief they please. *(Laughs with pleasure)*

(The witches join in the laughing and disappear into the forest)

Anne: Some months later I developed the mark of the Devil – a wart on my left knuckle. I was proud of that. It showed I was a true witch. It was then that I began to make pictures of clay, and the Devil began to talk to me.

(Anne goes off)

Potts: Witches often said they communicated with the Devil. A witch named Agnes Thompson is reported as stating –

Agnes: The Devil was clad in a black gown with a black hat upon his head. . . . His face was terrible, his nose like the beak of an eagle, great burning eyes; his hands and legs were hairy, with claws upon his hands, and feet like a griffon.

Potts: It is dangerous to meddle with such things. It's hard to stamp out this evil influence on our common folk. When once a witch joins a coven, it is as if she falls under a spell – poor wretch.

3 *Inside Malkin Tower*

Headline: Malkin Tower – the house of the witch, Mother Demdike.

Elizabeth Davies: The moon's high for the meeting, Mother.

Demdike: Elizabeth, we're to meet Christopher Holgate and his wife by the lake in Pendle Forest.

Elizabeth: Katherine Hewitt is late. Someone may have seen her on the way. I hope she's safe.

Demdike: After the last Sabbat she told me that she thinks her neighbours have suspicions.

Elizabeth: The people around are so set against us.

Demdike: Do not worry so, daughter. In our coven – there's our strength.

(Rhythmical tap at the door)

Demdike: Ah, Katherine Hewitt, you've come at last.

Elizabeth: Did anyone see you?

Katherine: Yes, I was followed to the crossroads, so I hid at the edge of the forest. That is why I'm late.

Elizabeth: Did they follow you here?

Katherine: No, I saw them return to the village.

Demdike: Good – then it's safe to begin! *(She laughs)*

Elizabeth: I've mixed the aconite and belladonna with the oil.

Demdike: Let us anoint ourselves.

(They rub on the oil and herbs and then begin to kneel round in a circle)

Elizabeth
Demdike
Katherine } : We call on the power of the spirits.

Demdike: Gather around us. Closer!

Elizabeth: Closer!

Katherine: Closer!

Demdike: Spirit called Tibb come ride with us.

Elizabeth: Spirit called Bull come ride with us.

Katherine: Spirit called Fancy come ride with us.

(They each stand, stretching out their arms, as the spirits arrive)

Elizabeth: It's getting darker.

Demdike: Now we shall leave swiftly. Help me, Elizabeth – my sight's not good today.

(They move with quick fleeting movements through the forest muttering the names of the spirits as they go. Sound of rustling leaves.)

Headline: By the lake in Pendle Forest.

(Christopher and Elizabeth Holgate emerge from the shadows and look round. Then Demdike, Elizabeth and Katherine arrive.)

Demdike: So you are here before us, Christopher Holgate. Welcome to our Sabbat meeting. Elizabeth . . . We have not seen you for some time! Are you both anointed?

Christopher: Yes we are.

Elizabeth Holgate: With the herbs I picked this afternoon.

Demdike: This is very good, and do you feel well?

Elizabeth Holgate: We are in good health, Mother Demdike.

(Enter Alice Gray, in a hurry and carrying a basket of food)

Demdike: Welcome, Alice Gray. Did you come alone?

Alice: Yes, Mother Demdike. I have brought the food.

Demdike: Are you sure you were not followed?

Alice: Yes – quite sure. I thought I heard voices further back, but all is quiet around here.

Demdike: Then we shall begin the Sabbat.

All: We are ready.

Demdike: Christopher Holgate, you are Chief Priest.

Christopher: Let us make the figures of clay.

(Sitting in a circle, each witch moulds a figure in clay chanting the name of a villager as she does so)

Christopher: Set the figures in the circle. *(He draws a symbolic circle and the witches place the figures in it)*

Christopher: Take the pins.

(They feet-stamp in ritual round the figures holding long pins up high and panting loudly)

Christopher: Pin the figures!

All: There . . . *(Slowly they push the pins in)* . . . in – they – go!

(They cry out in triumph and then fall back exhausted into a circle and sit)

Christopher: Here my friends, sup the hen's blood. Renew yourselves!

(He hands round the bowl of blood)

All: *(Supping)* Give us strength.

Demdike: Now we will feast. What have you prepared, Alice Gray?

Alice: We have mutton, wine and butter-milk, Mother Demdike.

Demdike: Let us eat and drink!

(Eating and drinking in slow ritual manner)

Demdike: That was good!

(Alizon, James and Jennet Davies emerge from the woods)

Elizabeth: Here are my children – Alizon, James and Jennet. They will join us now. Welcome to the Sabbat, children.

Demdike: Christopher Holgate, summon the spirits so that we can dance.

(He beats a rhythm on a tambourine. The witches stand and hold their arms up high. They dance to tambourine, fiddle and pipe music, or to their own chants. The dance ends in a frenetic climax. Then the witches shake hands together in a circle and swiftly leave the forest. Leaves rustle. Slowly and cautiously the gossips emerge from behind some trees.)

Knowall Gossip: Did you see it all?

Scared Gossip: It's evil, wicked.

Inquisitive Gossip: Who was that old woman?

Kn Gossip: That was old Mother Demdike.

Sympathetic Gossip: I know her. Her real name's Elizabeth Southern.

Sc Gossip: Don't have anything to do with her, she's the Devil's mouthpiece.

Inq Gossip: I thought I recognised the Holgate family. Didn't realise they had anything to do with old Demdike.

Kn Gossip: The others must have been her son and daughter.

Inq Gossip: And her grandchildren.

Sc Gossip: Did you see the woman's eyes?

Kn Gossip: Yes I did – one eye looks up . . .

Inq Gossip: And the other looks down! *(They laugh)*

Sc Gossip: Ugh! It gives me the shudders!

Inq Gossip: I'm sure I've seen some of them begging at Trawden Market.

Kn Gossip: They live at Malkin Tower, you know – not far from Greenhead. It's a strange house, I can tell you. Not that I'm in the habit of visiting the place that often!

Sc Gossip: We can't let the sort of thing we've seen go on.

Inq Gossip: No, we can't. You're right.

Symp Gossip: It's hard to tell. After all, Mother Demdike cured my lad's fever the other week. She gave me a herbal drink for him.

Inq Gossip: It's a wonder he didn't die!

Symp Gossip: I went to see her in desperation.

Kn Gossip: Witches spread disease; they don't get rid of it.

Symp Gossip: They mean well. My lad got better. I'm not the only one who goes to them for advice.

Sc Gossip: Did you see the way they plunged needles into those clay animals?

Inq Gossip: I thought they were clay people.

Sc Gossip: Well – their eyes went glassy – sort of dazed.

Kn Gossip: I reckon they was in a trance.

Sc Gossip: It makes me tremble!

Symp Gossip: Aye, it's eerie all right.

Kn Gossip: Shall we tell the priest?

Inq Gossip: Yes, and about that other old woman, Chattox. You know I told you I saw her in the Forest the other week. I reckon she's a witch too.

Kn Gossip: We'll watch them in the weeks to come and see if anything else happens.

Sc Gossip: And then we'll tell all about them.

Inq Gossip: Tell on them to the magistrate!

(Ayes of agreement. The gossips leave the forest looking nervously about them.)

Potts: There were two incidents which began the whole process of my official enquiry into witchcraft. The first involved Old Demdike and her daughter Elizabeth.

4 *Malkin Tower*

Headline: A room in Malkin Tower.

(Demdike and Elizabeth sit on stools finishing bowls of soup)

Elizabeth: Well, there wasn't much meat in that soup. I don't know what we're going to do for food tomorrow.

Demdike: Things are getting worse.

Elizabeth: We won't be able to afford meat for the next Sabbat.

Demdike: Have you finished the cleaning for Richard Baldwin, up at Wheathead Mill?

Elizabeth: Yes, Mother, but he won't be needing me any more. Not now that the new building is finished.

Demdike: He didn't want you for long then.

Elizabeth: It was hard work while it lasted. I don't think Baldwin liked me.

Demdike: How much did he pay you then? *(Pause)* Come on – out with it.

Elizabeth: One shilling.

Demdike: The old scoundrel! After working the skin off your bones! That's an insult. We'll have to go begging again. Curse the man!

Elizabeth: I know you don't see very well now, Mother, but could you not go and ask him for more money? I've tried and it's done no good. If you don't, we'll starve. There's no money in begging. Alizon will take you to Wheathead. She knows the way to Baldwin's house.

Demdike: All right. I'll go if I must. He deserves the Devil's curse.

Elizabeth: *(Calling)* Alizon! Alizon, come here will you! *(Alizon enters)* Lead your grandmother to Richard Baldwin's house. And mind you take care, her eyesight's getting worse.

Alizon: Come along, Grandma. Let me hold your arm. Now, this way.

(Demdike shuffles along with Alizon)

5 *The mill at Wheathead*

Demdike: Are we near the place yet?

Alizon: Yes, not far now. *(Sound of mill)* We're passing the mill. Watch the stones on this path. Careful! You'll stumble if you walk like that!

Demdike: Come on, come on lass, I can step out faster than this. Let go my arm!

Alizon: There's the house in the clearing ahead. *(Mr Baldwin and his daughter appear, looking at their garden)* And a man and a little girl's coming towards us.

Demdike: It must be Baldwin and his daughter.

Ellen Baldwin: Who's that old woman over there, Father?

Baldwin: The witch, Mother Demdike! Hey, you old hag! What do you want with me?

Demdike: We've come about the money you owe my daughter, Elizabeth Davies, for her hard labour.

Alizon: We've nothing left to eat, sir.

Demdike: Pay up, Baldwin.

Ellen: Please give them something, Father, they frighten me.

Baldwin: Get out of my grounds, old witch. And take the little hussy with you or I will burn the one of you and hang the other.

Demdike: Go hang thyself and curses be on thy head.

Baldwin: Come along, Ellen, let us return to the house. Quickly.

(Alizon and Demdike turn and go. Demdike shakes her fist.)

Potts: Very soon after this encounter, the miller's little daughter became ill, slowly declined and some weeks later died. She was buried at Colne.

(Churchyard. Bell tolling. Baldwin and Priest by grave. Village crowd.)

Priest: I commend thy soul to God the Father Almighty and thy body to the ground. . . . Earth to earth, ashes to ashes, dust to dust. May her spirit rest in peace.

Knowall Gossip: They say Old Demdike put a curse on her and that she died of shock.

Scared Gossip: All this evil talk is making me feel ill.

Inquisitive Gossip: It's not the first time the old hag has put curses on people.

Kn Gossip: Did you know that she has a spirit called Tibb? He's in the shape of a boy and wears a brown and black coat.

Inq Gossip: They say Demdike made a clay figure of Ellen Baldwin, then she dried it and stuck thorns in it – then it crumbled into pieces. Then Ellen died.

Sc Gossip: That's horrible! *(Frightened)* What's going to happen next?

(The gossips continue to gossip as Potts speaks)

Potts: There was a general murmuring of the populace, but no action was yet taken against the witches. Their begging continued to be tolerated, and their powers were still sought in healing sick cattle and people.

6 *The village of Colne*

Headline: 8th March 1612.

Potts: The second incident took place as Alizon Davies passed through the village of Colne on her way to Trawden Forest to beg.

(Villagers pass by on their way to market. Alizon Davies and John Law enter from different directions.)

Alizon: Hey there! Pedlar, will you stop? *(Calling)* I'd like to buy something.

John Law: My name's John Law, and I come from Halifax, and I can't be stopping for a wisp of a lass like yourself.

Alizon: But sir, I want to buy some pins. Please STOP.

John: I've not got time to undo my pack for the likes of you.

Alizon: STOP I tell you. I've every right to buy something from you if I want. Undo your pack!

John: That I won't, lass. I'm on my way to market. I haven't got time. Be off with you.

Alizon: I want some pins.

John: You want to steal some pins, I warrant.

Alizon: Don't you accuse me of being a thief.

John: Be on your way.

Alizon: I'll curse you for this.

John: Oh you will, will you? You little vixen!

(Sound of dog barking somewhere in the village)

Alizon: There's a good dog. There's a good boy! What would you have me do to that pedlar over there?

(Dog barking. John Law looks around, awkward and confused.)

Alizon: You can lame him? Good dog. *(Shouting)* A dog's curse be on you, John Law. *(To the dog)* Lame him then, boy! *(Dog barking)* Go on.

John: *(Staggering backwards)* Oh, my left arm. Oh the pain – it's shooting down my left side.

(John Law staggers off. Alizon runs off laughing in the other direction.)

Potts: At the exact moment that Alizon cursed him, John Law suffered a stroke. Whether it was coincidence or not I am unable to say. Roger Newell, a local magistrate, was responsible for the preliminary enquiries into these strange and disturbing incidents. He was a wealthy landowner and a firm believer in the influence that evil spirits could have over people.

7 *Courtroom at Read Hall*

Headline: 13th March 1612 Read Hall. The first official enquiry into witchcraft.

(Court officials and spectators assemble. Alizon Davies is led in.)

Nowell: We are assembled here at Read Hall to commence an official enquiry into the evil practice of witchcraft in and around the area of Pendle Forest in the County of Lancashire.

Alizon Davies – stand forward. Tell me frankly, Alizon Davies, how you became a witch.

Alizon: I'm not a witch. You shalt not say I am.

Nowell: There are people in the villages round here who say you are. Do you remember John Law? I've heard all about the incident. Who advised you to become a witch?

Alizon: No one. I am not a witch.

Nowell: Mother Demdike? Answer.

Alizon: No one.

Nowell: *(Trying a gentler approach)* Come now, you can't fool me, my dear. Your poor old grandmother, Demdike, has been a witch for years. You must have been with her.

Alizon: No, never. I've never been to her meetings.

Nowell: Ah – so you knew there were meetings.

Alizon: No, never.

Nowell: But you've just mentioned Demdike's meetings.

Alizon: No, I . . . *(She looks confused)*

Nowell: Did Demdike ask you to become a witch? Did she? If you do not answer you will be sent to prison, and there be shown the instruments of torture.

Alizon: *(After a pause)* Yes, she did.

Nowell: What acts of witchcraft have you seen her do?

Alizon: None.

Nowell: Hold her hands behind her back. *(The usher pins her arm)* So – what acts?

Alizon: She bewitched a cow. *(Looking round)* She charmed a can of milk so that a whole pound of butter appeared in it. *(Crowd murmurs)*

Nowell: What else? *(Usher twists her arms)*

Alizon: I saw Mother Demdike make a picture out of clay.

Nowell: Yes?

Alizon: It was a picture of Miller Baldwin's daughter.

Nowell: Go on. *(Arms twisted)*

Alizon: Then I saw her stab the picture with a needle and curse . . . again and again and again.

Nowell: And is this not the action of a witch?

Alizon: No – I mean yes.

Nowell: And now once again, Alizon Davies, I ask you – have YOU practised witchcraft?

Alizon: Yes I have.

Nowell: Thank you, Alizon Davies. You have done well to tell the truth. Now you will be imprisoned at Lancaster Castle and you will be tried with others of your kind for the wicked crime of witchcraft. Take her down.

(Crowd reaction. Drums in the distance.)

Headline: 2nd April 1612. The first enquiry ends.

Potts: On the evidence and confessions later obtained, Roger Nowell committed for trial –

Nowell: Demdike, Chattox and Anne Redfern.

Potts: They were sent – along with Alizon Davies – to Lancaster Gaol to await the August Assize. *(Distant drums)*

While they were in prison, a Sabbat meeting of twenty witches took place at Malkin Tower. They were betrayed and seized and the following persons committed to Lancaster:

Nowell: Elizabeth Davies, James Davies, Alice Nutter, Katherine Hewitt, Alice Gray, John Bulcock, Jane Bulcock. *(Distant drums)*

Potts: Mother Demdike, unable to endure for long the hardships of life in an overcrowded prison, took ill and died before the trial.

8 *Lancaster Assize Court. The jury, the court officials and public spectators assemble.*

Headline: 7th August 1612 – Lancaster Assize Court – the trial of the Pendle Witches begins.

Potts: The judges were Sir James Altham and Sir Edward Bromley.

Judge Bromley: Bring in the prisoners. *(They are led in by gaolers)*

Potts: Anne Whittle, otherwise known as Chattox, Elizabeth Davies, James Davies, Alizon Davies, Anne Redfern, Alice Nutter and Katherine Hewitt.

Judge Bromley: You are accused of witchcraft under the Witchcraft Act of 1604.

Judge Altham: If any person or persons . . . shall use, practice, or exercise any invocation, or conjuration, of any evil and wicked spirit, or shall consult, covenant with, entertain, feed, or reward any evil or wicked spirit to or for any intent or purpose: or . . . shall use, practice or exercise any witchcraft, enchantment, charm or sorcery . . . every such offender or offenders, being of any of the said offences duly and lawfully convicted . . . shall suffer pains of death as a felon or felons.

Judge Bromley: Anne Whittle, stand forward. Do you plead guilty or not guilty to the crime of witchcraft?

Chattox: Not guilty.

Judge Altham: Read out her confession – made voluntarily at Read Hall.

Nowell: Thirteen or fourteen years ago, after being instructed in the practice of witchcraft by Mother Demdike, a thing like a Christian man pestered me for my soul. I consented. He told me that my spirit was called Fancy. Very soon Fancy urged me to harm the wife of Richard Baldwin. When I refused, Fancy tried to bite my arm.

Judge Bromley: Do you acknowledge all this to be true?

Chattox: *(In tears)* I do. I beg for God's mercy, and for the forgiveness of my daughter, Anne Redfern.

Judge Bromley: Thank you, Anne Whittle. You may stand down.

Judge Altham: Elizabeth Davies, stand forward. You are charged with three murders by witchcraft. Do you plead guilty or not guilty?

Elizabeth: Not guilty.

Judge Bromley: It is said that you murdered John Robinson of Barley, his brother James, and Henry Mitton of Roughlee.

Elizabeth: None of this is true. It's all lies!

Nowell: Here is her voluntary confession made on 27th April 1612.

Judge Bromley: Let it be read.

Elizabeth: I don't want to hear it. You beat the confession out of me. *(Crowd murmurs)* I don't want . . .

Judge Bromley: Pray, silence in the courtroom. Elizabeth Davies, listen to your confession. Proceed, Justice Nowell.

Nowell: This is the voluntary confession of Elizabeth Davies: 'I confess that I have a spirit named Bull which comes to me as a brown dog. In the year 1608 John Robinson of Barley accused me of having a child out of wedlock – so I made a picture of clay at the west end of Malkin Tower. I dried it by a fire and crumbled it. Within a week John Robinson died. I also confess that with the help of my mother, Demdike, and with the help of Alice Nutter, I bewitched Henry Mitton.'

Elizabeth: You villains! I confessed while you stretched my arms and legs to breaking point on the rack! You're all liars!

Judge Altham: Two of your children, James and Jennet, have witnessed against you.

Elizabeth: A hundred curses on them!

Judge Bromley: Read out the statement made by James Davies.

Nowell: 'On Good Friday in the year 1610 I killed a sheep to provide dinner for my mother, Elizabeth Davies, who met with other witches at Malkin Tower to baptise my sister Alizon in the name of the Devil. They plotted to blow up Lancaster Castle and kill Mr Lister of Westby.'

Elizabeth: That's all lies. LIES!

Judge Bromley: Silence!

Nowell: Now I call on Jennet Davies to give evidence.

Judge Bromley: Jennet Davies – stand upon that table.

Elizabeth: Get my daughter out of this courtroom. I don't want to see her. Get her out!

(Crowd chatters loudly)

Get her out! A curse be on her!

Judge Bromley: Silence! Remove Elizabeth Davies. *(Gaolers come forward)*

Elizabeth: That's right – take me back to the foul, stinking dungeons where my mother died. Leave me there to rot in the dark and damp.

Judge Bromley: Remove her! *(Gaolers handle her roughly and take her out)*

Elizabeth: *(Calling)* Curses be on you all.

Nowell: Jennet Davies, what evidence have you that your mother is a witch?

Judge Bromley: Don't be afraid. We only want the truth. Speak, my child.

Jennet: I know my mother to be a witch. I have seen her spirit come to our home at Malkin Tower, in the likeness of a brown dog. She used this spirit to kill John Robinson from the village of Barley. She also killed James Robinson and

Henry Mitton. She used to meet hundreds of witches in a coven at our house and in Pendle Forest.

Nowell: That will be all, Jennet. You may step down.

Judge Altham: Bring back Elizabeth Davies.

(Crowd mutters. The gaolers bring her in. Elizabeth mutters.)

Elizabeth: Let my children hang me not. *(Quietly)* The Devil take their souls. *(Almost crying)*

Judge Bromley: Stand up, Elizabeth Davies.

Elizabeth: You've made Jennet witness against me. *(Louder)* She's frightened out of her wits.

Judge Bromley: Elizabeth Davies, do you now wish to confess to the evil crime of witchcraft?

Elizabeth: I will not confess to the crime of witchcraft.

(Some of the crowd shout abuse)

Judge Bromley: CONFESS!

Elizabeth: *(Quietly)* I will not – but *(There is complete silence)* . . . I beg the court for mercy. *(Exhausted)*

(Murmuring of crowd)

Potts: The trials lasted for three days. John Bulcock and his mother, Jane, were acquitted for lack of evidence.

Headline: 19th August.

Judge Bromley: Members of the jury, you have listened carefully to all the confessions and evidence concerning the most terrible accusations of witchcraft in the County of Lancashire. Do you wish to have time to consider your verdict? *(Jury confer and then shake their heads)* No? Then you find these persons guilty or not guilty?

Jury: GUILTY!

Judge Altham: Prisoners, stand.

Judge Bromley: You are all found guilty of the most wicked and unforgivable crime of witchcraft. *(He puts the black square on his head)* You shall all go from hence, to the castle whence you came. From thence you shall be carried to the place of Execution for this county, where your bodies shall be hanged until you are dead. And God have mercy upon your souls. *(Drum beat)*

9 *The courtyard of Lancaster Castle. The witches are led through the crowds who have come to watch the hangings.*

Headline: 20th August.

(Low drum beating)

Knowall Gossip: There they are – the demons. Down with them.

(The crowd takes up the chant)

Sympathetic Gossip: God have mercy on them.

Inquisitive Gossip: The Devil take their souls.

Kn Gossip: Let them burn in hell-fire.

Symp Gossip: They're innocent women and children.

Scared Gossip: I've seen a Sabbat meeting – they meet the Devil.

Kn Gossip: And they drink their victims' blood.

Symp Gossip: Don't you remember – Demdike cured my son?

Inq Gossip: Witch lover!

Kn Gossip: Let's get her!

Inq Gossip: Let's hang her too!

(They run to the woman and start to beat her)

Symp Gossip: Mercy – save me. I'm only telling the truth.

(Guards rescue the woman)

Some of the crowd: Go on – hang them.

Guard: Come on – up here, witches. Vermin!

(The guards take the witches to the gibbets)

Crowd chant: Hang them!

(Drums beat to a climax. Silence.)

Symp Gossip: They're dead.

(The crowd slowly disperses)

Scapegoat

by Michael Maynard

Cast:

Gary
Liz
Jana's Computer
Jana
President of Zaria
President of Earth
Chief of Ruling Council
Outspoken Councillor
Forecasting Executive
Forward Planning Executive
Information Executive
Employment Executive
Earthling Interviewee
Zarian Interviewee
Interviewer
Speaker
Dana
Andrai
Glen
Praham
Soolene
Child
Mum
Zarian 1
Zarian 2
Zarian Crowd
Earthling Crowd
Flight Computer

Gary enters holding something resembling a small cassette recorder. It also has what looks like a small TV screen. He is inspecting it with interest. His older sister Liz enters.

Liz: What you nicked this time, Gary?

Gary: Nothing.

Liz: What's that then? Scotch mist?

Gary: No, I found it.

Liz: Oh yeah, where? Shop window or back of a lorry?

Gary: Give over. It was just lying around on the waste ground.

Liz: What is it?

Gary: Dunno.

Liz: Give it here. *(She grabs at it)*

Gary: No. Get off.

(They struggle. There's a click sound and then a strange noise comes from the object.)

Liz: Hey listen.

Gary: You pressed that knob.

Liz: I didn't, you did.

Gary: Sshh.

(The strange electronic sounds change into a voice . . .)

Computer Voice: This is a distress data recording. Please activate the tape cartridge. Whoever, wherever, whenever you are . . . please activate the tape cartridge.

Gary: What?

Liz: Press that knob there. Go on.

(Gary does so. Another electronic sound denoting that the tape has been activated.)

Computer Voice: Thank you. The tape cartridge has now been activated. This machine is a life recreator. You will now see a visual representation. Here is the motivator of this space log.

Gary: Hey look, there's a picture.

(They stare at the screen. We now see, acted out in a separate area, what they are viewing on the screen. Gary and Liz remain as a link between events on stage and the audience.)

Jana: Whoever you are, I thank you for at last triggering the mechanism to replay this data record cartridge. No matter what time-zone or solar system you inhabit, you must please watch this visual log of my experiences on the planet Zarius. But first I must tell you of myself. My name is Jana Heleana 7TX. 7TX is my family and planet code number. My friends just say Jana. I'm thirteen Earth-years old. I am a Zarian, though my parents were born on Earth . . . in the Europe zone. I have made this log so that my experiences should not be forgotten. I believe that I am the only survivor of the disaster.

Computer: Affirmative. Sole survivor Jana Heleana 7TX. Data cartridge section two ready for activation. *(Tone)* Second section activated. Jana Heleana 7TX will now recall the historical background to this log.

Jana: Thank you. As I said, my parents lived on Earth and life there in the twenty-first century could be pretty good for some. This was all before I was born. The planet prospered and most were content. . . . Until the visitation.

Computer: Visitation in the 'Earth-year' two thousand and twenty-six. Visitors: Zarians.

Jana: Yes, the Zarians had mastered space and time travel and came from their planet many light years away in a different solar system. They are similar to human beings, which is why they chose Earth, but the only difference is their skin . . .

(Zarians begin to appear in a separate area)

. . . which is rather like polythene. Quite clear and see-through. And the two, almost identical planets became trading partners.

Computer: Instant playback, histo recording. Exhibit Alpha.

(An Earthling of the twenty-first century steps forward to greet a Zarian)

President: I, on behalf of the citizens of United Earth, welcome this treaty with the Zarian people.

Chief: I, as the Chief Executive of the Zarian Ruling Council, welcome Earth as our new colony and partner. We look forward to years of fruitful exchange between our two great planets.

Computer: Exhibit Alpha terminated.

Jana: Two Earth-years before I was born, the Zarians invited us Earth people to go and live on their planet. It came as a great and generous sign of friendship. But I think there was more to it than that . . .

Computer: Histo-recording, Exhibit Beta.

(A meeting of the Zarian Ruling Council)

Chief: The Ruling Council is now in session. The Employment Executive, please.

Employment Exec: Thank you. As you know, our planet is rich in minerals. Although our technology is advancing, we are still unable to extract as much of the mineral deposits as we could sell on the inter-planetary market.

Others: 'Hear, hear', 'I agree', etc.

Chief: Problem understood. Proposed solution?

Employment Exec: We need more workers. Then we could get more minerals out, sell more, and thus increase our gross planetary profit.

Others: 'Hear, hear', 'Good', etc.

Chief: Where do you suggest we get this enlarged work force?

Employment Exec: One of our companion colonies, Earth, has a lot of cheap labour. If we invited them here, gave them Zarian citizenship, then they could share in our new wealth.

Others: 'I agree', 'Good idea', etc.

Computer: Exhibit Beta terminated.

Jana: Well, whatever the reasons, thousands accepted the offer, including my parents. They obtained passbook visas and became Zarian citizens. They were excited at the prospect of living on Zarius and looked forward to a golden future. However, all was not quite as wonderful as they'd imagined. When they arrived they found life was a bit difficult. Food was expensive and my parents had to work extra-time to afford a nice living-unit. They had to learn new ways and different customs. Eventually they got established and I was born. For the next eleven Earth-years the Zarian economy flourished and all went well. But then things started to go wrong.

Computer: Instant playback, histo-record, Exhibit Gamma.

(We see a television news reporter in a futuristic mould, but retaining the 'newshound' attitude)

Announcer: Since the planet-quake last season, mineral deposits have been buried and reserves are low. Much of the wealth of the planet has been lost and it looks as if hard times are on the way. Many will lose their jobs. Has the Ruling Council slipped up this time? Is this a giant blunder or is there an explanation?

Computer: Exhibit Gamma terminated.

Jana: There was much discontent as the situation worsened, and people found it difficult to live as comfortably as they'd done before.

Computer: Histo-recording Exhibit Delta.

(The Ruling Council meet. Though predominantly old, they behave like squabbling infants.)

Chief: Order, order please. I call this meeting of the Ruling Council to order. Quiet please. *(Quiet)* Thank you. Let's re-cap. Problem analysis?

Council Computer: Planet-quake buried 20% of mineral wealth beyond reach. Safety measures inadequate. Provisions unsatisfactory. Mismanagement and bad planning. Millions now unemployed.

Outspoken Councillor: Why were there no advance warning forecasts of the quake?

Forecasting Exec: As Executive of the Forecasting Department, I resent that attack. Such disturbances are extremely difficult to predict. Why didn't Foreward Planning anticipate this eventuality and remove deposits from the risk area beforehand? They're to blame. *(General uproar)*

Foreward Planning: Not true, we did our best. We could only recover 4% of the threatened deposits, because the Works Department were too slow in delivery of the required back-up equipment. It's their fault. *(Uproar)*

Outspoken Councillor: Look, why don't you admit it, you're *all* responsible.

Others: 'Nonsense', 'Ridiculous', 'I'm not to blame', etc.

Chief: Perhaps we are all to blame. But the question now is: what are we going to do about it? Suggestions please.

Outspoken Councillor: I think you should all resign and we'll have an election immediately. *(No . . . No . . .)* Meanwhile Forward Planning should organise things so that we can all live with fewer minerals. *(No . . . No . . .)* Why not? Do you think you've got too much to lose to admit mistakes? *(Uproar)*

Information Exec: Wait. I think I've got a plan. Yes, we *are* all responsible, but it's pointless telling the mass of people that, when they'd much rather believe something else.

Others: What do you mean? Explain.

Information Exec: Our analysis of people is that they dislike difference. They are suspicious of things strange to them. They are unwilling to accept strangers and newcomers.

Chief: Please come to the point.

Information Exec: I suggest 'Operation Scapegoat'.

Others: Scapegoat?

Info Exec: Yes, scapegoat. And I think we've got the ideal group to blame.

Others: *(Excited)* You mean the Earthling settlers?

Info Exec: Yes.

Chief: But how?

Info Exec: Just use the fact that most people think they don't belong here . . .

Outspoken Councillor: But that's ridiculous; we invited them here . . . encouraged them to come.

Info Exec: People have short memories.

Outspoken Councillor: But they've made their homes here. Many of them were born here. They couldn't go back now even if they wanted to. They are as much Zarian citizens as you or I . . .

Info Exec: All that might be true, but people would rather find others to blame.

Chief: And the Earthlings are an ideal group. They've recently arrived, they look different, it's easy to pick them out . . . Yes, I think you've got something here.

Info Exec: We need to find ways of stirring up a little resentment. Show how they've caused trouble. I'll get my people at the Department of Information to think up some ways of spreading the poison.

(They freeze in a position that expresses their reaction to the plan)

Computer: Instant play-back histo-recording, Exhibit Epsilon.

(The setting is a futuristic 'Nuremburg/National Front' rally)

Speaker: Friends. Many of you wonder why this great planet of ours has got problems. Perhaps it is not as great as it was . . .

Crowd: *(Protest)* No . . .

Speaker: What can have gone wrong? Who's to blame for all this? Some say that you, the citizens of Zarius, are at fault. But how can you be? You all work hard, and are loyal to our fine planet. So who . . . who's to blame? I will tell you. There are amongst us beings who do not belong here: aliens who look different, behave differently, have different ways of life. Why? Because they *are* different. They don't belong here. They are foreign to us. We are pure beings. Our skin is clear; not coloured white or brown or pink or yellow. No, we are pure. We mustn't be contaminated by this disease in our society. These alien Earthlings with their strange skins and primitive ways should be sent back to Earth. They should be banished from our planet. There's not enough space for them. Zarius for the Zarians!

Crowd: Zarius for the Zarians!

Speaker: We can get back to the way we were, if we get rid of them. They're nothing but primitive beasts, no better than animals. Draining our strength and purity. Send them home. Get them out.

Crowd: Out. Out. Out . . .

Computer: Exhibit Epsilon terminated.

Jana: I could understand the elders agreeing with that kind of speech, but I couldn't believe that the younger people would take any notice of it. Certainly not friends at the club centre . . .

Computer: Instant playback histo-recording Exhibit Zeta . . .

(Youth club. Electronic pop musak. Young teenagers.)

Andrai: Hey, did you hear about the rally?

Praham: Yes. My unit elders said they thought it all the time. 'Never should have let the Earthlings in, in the first place', they said.

Glen: Sooner we get rid of them, the better.

Dana: I always said they were funny. Little Earthies.

Andrai: 'Cos of the weird food they eat.

Dana: Ever tried it?

Glen: No fear.

Praham: Steak and kidney pie?

All: Ugh! Hahaha.

Glen: Chop suey.

All: Ugh.

Andrai: Kee-bab!

(They all laugh)

Dana: Fish and chips!!

(They all fall about with laughing and pretend vomiting.)

Andrai: No wonder their skin's the way it is.

Glen: They must be more primitive than us. Less developed.

Dana: Yeah, just down from the trees.

Praham: Ought to bury 'em back in the Earth . . .

All: Earthies. Ugh.

Jana: *(Commenting on the scene)* The only person who stood up for me was my best friend Soolene Nola 3DX. She was my next-unit neighbour. Soolene was one of the few to answer back.

(Back to the youth club)

Soolene: Do you believe all this?

Dana: What do you mean, Soolene?

Soolene: Well, how can you agree with all those lies?

Andrai: Lies?

Soolene: Well, you know for yourselves that half of what was said isn't true.

Glen: We know Earthies are weird all right.

Soolene: How can you say that? Some of your best friends are Earthlings. What about Jana? Is she weird and odd?

Praham: It's different with her. She's all right.

Glen: It's the rest of them.

Dana: Sooner we get rid of them the better.

Soolene: How can you be so horrible?

Dana: *(Mocking)* Ah, you feel sorry for them, do you?

Andrai: Yes, be kind to the little animals.

Praham: Earthies are all right . . . as pets. *(They laugh)*

Soolene: They're no different from us. Why can't we just carry on, sharing our life here together?

Andrai: *(Vicious)* 'Cos they're dangerous, that's why. You heard the elders. They all agree. It was a mistake to let the scum in.

(The scene ends in uproar)

Computer: Exhibit Zeta terminated.

Jana: Things were beginning to get out of hand. People weren't thinking, they were just being . . . unreasonable . . .

Computer: Instant playback histo-recording Eta . . .

(A TV studio)

Interviewer: In the studio this half-day we have representatives of the Earthlings' Equal Rights Campaign, and members of the New Association of 'Zarius for the Zarians' Party. Now I turn first to the Earthlings to outline their grievances.

Earthling: I think people looked around for why things were going wrong. And instead of *really* thinking about the situation and what should be done, they wanted an easy answer. . . someone to blame. All I can think of is that we're the odd ones out. Therefore an easy group to pick on.

Interviewer: Now let's hear from the Zarians. Are you 'just picking on' the Earthlings because they're different?

Zarian: Well, they certainly are different. They have their own ways; they eat and speak differently . . . even look different. They have no place here.

Earthling: I suppose you want only people who are identical to you. You'll be picking on *any* differences next. People who are short, or with squints, or those who are left-handed . . . anybody. Why are you making us a scapegoat for your problems?

Zarian: Look, face it, you *are* at fault. We can't get work or units to live in. There're not enough jobs to go round. Earthies are pinching our jobs and our homes.

Earthling: What do you mean, *we're* pinching them? There're more of us out of work and homeless than anyone.

Zarian: We were all right till you got here . . .

Earthling: You were all right *after* we came too. We prospered for years together. The present problems aren't our fault . . .

Interviewer: I'm sorry, time has beaten us. I'm sure this debate will continue between people all over the planet, but now it's time for a promotional interlude . . .

(A futuristic advert)

Child: Oh Mum, I'm hungry. Can't we eat now?

Mum: OK, what would you like?

Child: Some Vitaprotum please.

Mum: *(Emptying some 'Smartie'-type pills)* Here we are. Vitaprotum, the complete diet in a choice of colours.

Child: Yellow for me, please . . . Yummy yummy.

Mum: Here we are: condensed sheep. The protein from six animals condensed into one tasty pill. No wonder it's their favourite.

Interviewer: And now it's time for a news events data announcement.

Newsreader: The Ruling Council have just implemented a new Nationality Legislation, classifying Earthlings as second-class citizens immediately. There have been riots throughout their living regions. Protests by Earthlings led to mobs of mainly unemployed Zarians carrying out mass beatings. Many Earthlings have been injured, others have been thrown out of their living units.

Earthling crowd: We demand our rights! Why should we be treated like this? Back to equality now!

Zarian crowd: Zarius for the Zarians! Zarius for the Zarians! Look, there's some there. Let's get them. Earthies out, Earthies out! Earthies out, out, out!

(A stylised, perhaps slow-motion, fight takes place with beating and screaming, etc. Jana finds Soolene.)

Jana: Soolene, there you are. What's going on?

Soolene: Can't you see. The mobs are rounding up all the Earthlings and forcing them into spaceships. They're going to send them off the planet.

Jana: But they can't. Those ships aren't powerful enough to take the load. They'll be destroyed.

Soolene: I know, but one's already been sent off. No, look, it hasn't gone yet. It's there, just taking off.

(We hear the sound of a rocket launch)

Soolene: Look, there it goes. Yes, it's going to make it . . .

(Followed by an explosion)

Soolene: Oh no. The strain on the booster jets was too great.

Jana: They didn't stand a chance.

Zarian 1: Serves them right. *(Laughs)*

Zarian 2: Hear the way they scream. Just like animals. *(Laughs)*

Zarian 1: Better than a firework display.

Jana: How can they talk like that about people being killed?

Soolene: Come on, we must get away from here.

Jana: But my parents, what about them?

Soolene: I'm sorry, Jana, but I saw them earlier being dragged away by a crowd. I think they've already been put aboard a ship.

Jana: I must go and find them . . .

Soolene: No . . .

Jana: *(Bumping into a Zarian)* Oh sorry.

Zarian 1: You will be, little Earthy, when we've finished with you. *(Grabs her: Jana screams)*

Zarian 2: Oh, does it hurt? Poor little thing.

Soolene: Leave her alone.

Zarian 2: Mind your own business.

(Soolene kicks the Zarian and Jana escapes. They run off.)

Zarian 1: Come on, let's catch them.

(They too run off. Zarian 2 is hobbling. Soolene and Jana, out of breath, creep on.)

Soolene: Come on, Jana, through this doorway here.

Jana: Great – it's empty.

(The Zarians are shouting as they follow)

Soolene: They're right behind us. We must hide.

Jana: Here. Quick. *(They hide)*

Zarian 2: They must be here somewhere.

Zarian 1: She's only an Earthy, they can't run very fast, can they?

Zarian 1: We must find her. We've got to get rid of all of them. Otherwise the contamination will still be around.

Zarian 2: Right. Clean the planet of their filth. They must be round the back. Come on, keep up.

Zarian 1: I'm tired of running.

Zarian 2: Don't be so Earthy. Come on, let's look over there.

(They go)
(Soolene and Jana emerge from their hiding place)

Soolene: I think they've gone.

Jana: Oh Soolene, what am I going to do?

Soolene: We must get you away from here. Look, my elders have got an old private ship. It's small, but it might work. You'll have to go off in that.

Jana: But I couldn't . . .

Soolene: There's no choice.

(They run off)

Computer: Exhibit Eta terminated. Instant playback histo-recording Theta. On board the space ship.

(Jana sits at the controls)

Jana: I've never piloted one of these before.

Soolene: It's easy. Here's the computer. It's fully programmed. I'll just switch it to auto-rocket. You'll hardly have to do anything.

Jana: All right, I'll try.

Flight Computer: Auto-rocket activated. Five marks to ignition. Please activate fuel feed.

Jana: Where is it?

Soolene: Here. Go on. There's a crowd coming this way.

(We hear noises of the crowd in the distance)

Flight C: Fuel feed pumping. Three marks to ignition.

(Sound of engines)

Jana: I don't suppose many have survived?

Soolene: No . . . Goodbye, Jana. Hey, and make sure you let people know what's happened.

Flight C: Two marks to ignition.

Jana: Bye, Soolene. Thanks.

Flight C: One mark to ignition. Stand by, please.

(The sound of the crowd builds and mixes with the sound of the rocket engine. They stop abruptly.)

Computer: Exhibit Theta terminated.

Jana: Yes, I just managed to escape the worst, and now you know the whole story. As far as I know, I am the only survivor, and I don't know how long I'll be able to live. But I have made the cartridge so that people will know what led to this and . . .

Computer: Warning. Life support systems critical.

Jana: Who knows what will happen? I only hope that I can . . .

Computer: Serious malfunction. Termination situation.

(The area in which Jana has appeared goes dead, e.g. lights to blackout)

Liz: Oh, the picture's gone.

Gary: *(Shaking the recorder)* That's it. It's broken.

Liz: It's all over.

Gary: Good, weren't it?

Liz: Yeah, amazing.

Gary: Could never happen here though, could it?

(He runs off leaving Liz holding the recorder)

Liz: *(Thoughtfully)* Couldn't it?

Notes to the plays

Oi You Kids!

Conflict between young and old – 'It wasn't like that in my young day' – is nothing new, but this play looks at the conflict in an interesting way. After all, who is the scapegoat here – the one who takes the blame? Don't Danny and his friends make Mr Steadman the scapegoat of their escapades – and doesn't he make them scapegoats too? This is something you might like to discuss.

The characters

You need to work out the differences in attitude between the three members of the 'gang' – Danny, Jane and Steve. It's clear who is the most active – the leader – but is there any point where you would say that Danny is anything other than totally self-centred? In the last scene, do you think he shows a glimmer of awareness of how Mr Steadman feels? If you agree that he does, then the actor playing Danny must find a way of showing this change.

What about Jane? Would you say she is good at finding solutions to the gang's problems, or does she just try to creep round people? Can you find lines in the play where Jane shows that she is capable of being sympathetic to other people's points of view?

Steve may seem to you a bit of a coward. After all, he won't play knock-down-ginger. But is this because he knows when a game has gone far enough – because he believes that 'discretion is the better part of valour'? Whatever you decide about Steve, does it fit in with the fact that later on he seems to change his mind and agrees to help Danny 're-arrange' the gnomes? You may need to spend some time working this out if you are rehearsing the play for performance. (Incidentally, you may know knock-down-ginger – the game of knocking on people's letterboxes and running away – by another name. If so, use your name in the script.)

Mr Steadman's part is probably the hardest for you – after all, you may well find yourself agreeing with Danny! Try to recall all you can about old people, particularly your own relatives. When do you enjoy their company and when not? Imagine your own nan or grandpa having to put up with a boy like Danny. How would they react to him? You could improvise such a scene as a way of building up the characters.

The important thing in acting is to get inside the mind of the character you are playing. Otherwise you may concentrate too much on 'externals' – like imagining all old people with bent backs, walking sticks and croaky voices. (Which is probably what Danny does.) It's more helpful to work out how your particular character of an old man feels. Then you can start to develop the way he speaks and moves. Would you agree that Mr Steadman's bad temper is more important to the way the play develops than his actual age?

The same kind of thing is true for the mum. Put yourself in your own mum's shoes and imagine dealing with Danny. Perhaps you have a younger brother to model him on. When you have explored such a situation – perhaps with improvisations – you should deliberately try to remember some of the feelings you have gone through, so that you can draw on them as you act the mum.

Staging

The main action takes place in the street. But you need to show a number of places:

The street
Mr Steadman's front gate, garden path, front door, hallway and living room
A wall or hedge for Danny to hide behind
Danny's kitchen with table and chairs
A shed

If you are acting the play in a drama lesson, all of these areas can be represented with chairs and rostra-blocks.

For performance, some kind of in-the-round or avenue shape would probably be best. For example:

←— — — — — — — — Audience — — — — — — — —→

shed/kitchen street gate door Mr Steadman's house

←— — — — — — — — Audience — — — — — — — —→

Lights and sound

Lighting is not essential, but drama groups may like to spotlight the different areas and brighten them as the action moves from one place to another. If you can colour the light, use a bluer light for outdoors and a warmer light for indoors.

You will need to represent the crash of breaking glass – it's a very important part of the drama. You may be able to get suitable effects on disc, otherwise you will have to record the sound yourself. But take *great care* and have an adult in charge. When we recorded the play for BBC School Radio, the sound engineers set up an old pane of glass against a wall in a quiet corner of a school playground and put a microphone on a stand a metre or so away. We all stood well back, and the boy playing Danny threw a half-brick at the glass from several metres back. We had to do it three times – three panes of glass – to get it right, and spent a long time clearing up with dustpans and brushes. We wore gardening gloves for safety. It's a fun thing to do, but make sure no one else is around (we were recording during a school holiday), and see that an adult is in full control of the situation.

Another, safer way, is to simulate the crash of glass by dropping a set of thin metal plates on cue. The metalwork teacher may be able to help you. Alternatively, for classroom work without an audience, you might agree simply to crash a cymbal. It's the right *dramatic* sound even if it's not right realistically.

A disc or your own recording made in a street or a garden could usefully help to distinguish between the indoor and outdoor scenes.

Tape and video recording

The play will work well in either medium. For the BBC sound production we recorded the play indoors and outdoors at a school in Aldershot. If you cannot work on location, background sounds are important to distinguish between indoors and outdoors.

Video recording would cry out for location work. Perhaps there's a cul-de-sac which could be used, or part of the school grounds. The important thing is not to annoy other people or obstruct them. The milkman, for instance, won't be too pleased to find a video camera set up in the middle of his milk round!

You would probably have to fake the breaking windows. One way is to cut from a shot of the ball being kicked to a broken pane of glass. This could be simulated by cutting cracks and a jagged hole in an acetate sheet which is fixed across the window.

You will of course need to prepare a camera script showing the shots. There are books on video recording which explain how to do this.

Discussion and follow-up

1 Who would you say is/are the scapegoat(s) in this play?

2 How reasonable is the behaviour of Danny and the behaviour of Mr Steadman?

3 How much do you think the conflict is one of personalities, or because Danny and his friends lack play facilities? You might like to make a comparison with the situation of the young people in *A Straight Choice*, a play in the companion volume *Upheavals?*

4 If you were a town planner, would you segregate old people's and family housing – that is, keep them well apart? Or would you argue that there are good reasons for planning housing so as to bring different ages together?

Draw a plan for a new housing development according to your views. Present the plan to the rest of your group or class who could play the role of councillors on a planning committee.

5 Discuss situations where you've quarrelled with older people. Improvise the situations, or write them as scenes, and act them out. Can you devise them in such a way that the older characters have as good a say – and as good parts – as the youngsters?

6 Why should we try to see the other person's point of view? Can you imagine and write about or role-play societies in which everyone is totally self-centred? What is the outcome – and the ending of your story or play?

Don't be a Durr

'Durrbrain' is the unpleasant nickname for someone who appears not to be very bright, which is used in some parts of England. Where you live, there may be a different name, and you may wish to use that instead (and change the title of the play).

The play is written in Cockney dialect. You may prefer to change it into your own local dialect. After all, the point of the play applies anywhere. If you do this, some phrases may have to be changed, for instance 'a trip up West'. In London, this means going to the West End, where most entertainments are to be found. You'll need to change this to refer to your local entertainment spot.

Acting the characters

The intention of the play is to look closely at the attitudes of people who put others down by using unpleasant nicknames. This makes Gary's part the most difficult, because he has got to put up with a lot of abuse. For this reason, the play is best read or performed by groups of very good friends, and Gary should be performed by the most confident of them.

Inventive groups may like to have a different actor playing Gary in each scene – perhaps using a simple half-mask. If you do this, you might like to ask yourselves afterwards what extra meaning is then given to the play.

In this play, you need to think carefully about where the audience's sympathies are meant to lie. It may be that at the beginning the audience should find Marilyn and Zoe the characters they like best, and they should see Gary through the two girls' eyes. By the end, though, the audience should realise that Gary is the more likeable person, despite his superficial handicap, and that Zoe, and especially Marilyn, are cruel and heartless.

Miss Norton, the teacher, needs careful playing. Try to

decide from her words what sort of person she is. You may be tempted to model the character on a teacher in your school, but this will throw the play off-balance. (Why – what will be the effect on your audience?) At the end, do you think Miss Norton enjoys putting Marilyn in her place?

Those of you who play Mum, Dad, Gary and Stuart, need to sort out how your character treats each one of the others. In particular, discuss how the Dad treats Gary, and why Gary doesn't answer. What is Gary feeling? Stuart often seems to ignore Dad's remarks. Is this rudeness or something else? Can you say what you think it is?

The bus and classroom scenes need extra non-speaking parts to be improvised in.

Staging

Several areas are needed: the bus
the classroom
Gary's home with table and chairs
the cafe with video games

At the simplest, you could set up groups of chairs to represent all these areas, and simply move between them. Alternatively, you could set up two double rows of chairs to be both bus and classroom, and chairs and table for home and shop. In-the-round, or on a stage – if you are planning a performance – the chairs could be carried on or off for each scene by the actors taking part.

The video game is important for the opportunity it gives Gary to turn the tables on Marilyn. You could use a box or a television set, or you may be able to use a real video game. If not, sound effects will be necessary, and perhaps you could record these from a home computer.

If you are able to use simple lighting, this can be dimmed between scenes, especially where you need to suggest a time lapse.

Discussion and follow-up

1 Examine Marilyn's jokes and make sure you understand how they get their humour. What do you feel

about jokes that poke fun at others' weaknesses? What does Marilyn feel?

2 What do Marilyn, Zoe and Dad have in common? How much are they responsible for the way Gary is?

3 Discuss the idea that people learn to play the role which others cast them in. For example, if you are told frequently enough that you are a failure, do you fail deliberately in order to fit?

4 Discuss the way the student treats Gary. How does it differ from the way the others treat him?

5 Write diaries of the events of the play, as if you were Gary, Marilyn, or the student.

6 Is the teacher, Miss Norton, sufficiently aware of what is happening in her class? Should she do more to help Gary, or would that be favouritism?

7 Write a school report on Gary (i) before the play begins (ii) after the events of the play.

8 Have you ever poked fun at others? Try to answer honestly! – and have you had fun poked at you? Is that the way life is, or can we change things?

9 Write or improvise your own plays about people turning the tables on those who ridicule them.

The Pendle Witches

This play is based on real events which took place some three hundred and fifty years ago. The dialogue is based on records written at the time, and because of this use of old documents, the play could be called a 'documentary'.

The main characters really existed, and by gleaning scraps of information from the records the playwright has pieced together the kind of person that each one was. Old Chattox really did mumble, and Alizon Davies really did betray the other witches under pressure in the court room.

The characters

There are really three groups of characters in this play, the witches (both women and men), the gossips, and the judges and officials of the courts.

The judges were harsh men when it came to dealing with poor people like those who lived in the wretched villages around Pendle Forest in Lancashire. The first fifteen years of the seventeenth century had seen many upheavals in Britain, and those in authority were stamping law and order into ordinary people all over the country. The price of corn – and therefore of bread – had been going up and up until the hungry people rioted. Parliament and the King had narrowly escaped being blown up by Guy Fawkes, and the Catholic religion had been outlawed. In all these events the authorities thought they saw the work of the Devil, and especially in anything that involved witchcraft. They thought they were carrying out God's work on earth, and they did so with King James's blessing. He had spent seven years researching and writing a book about demons and witches and in 1604 severe new laws were passed, under which many witches were rounded up and burnt.

What we know about the witches is mainly based on what their enemies wrote. But if you allow for the anti-witch hysteria of the time, what comes out is a picture not of groups of Satan worshippers digging up graves at midnight, nor long-toothed hags riding broomsticks, but rather a number of women and some men who, although very poor, were successful practitioners of herbal medicine. Their knowledge must have been handed down over generations, and as modern science finds out more and more about the use of plant materials as a source of drugs it becomes harder to scorn them. They used foxglove extracts, just as modern medicine does, to control heart disease. They may even have experienced flying – at least in their minds – for the aconite and belladonna which they rubbed into their skins can cause the sensation of flying. These plants contain substances which are highly poisonous, but in minute quantities cause hallucinations.

These witches, then, were effectively the local nurses or doctors. People went to them for cures, which in all probability worked – or at least worked better than the standard 'cure' of the time, which was extracting blood with live leeches. If they also met in groups called 'covens', made sacrifices, and danced themselves into a frenzy we might say that was their own business. There is no real evidence that their curses harmed anyone – the deaths in this play could equally well have had natural causes. And no doubt the authorities also enjoyed dancing and drinking wine.

The third group of characters, the gossips, are invented. But they represent the range of attitudes which common people at the time must have felt, so they are not fictitious. The sympathetic gossip must have been helped by the witches; the malicious gossip is at the other extreme.

Acting the parts

In all documentary plays, characters should be acted with clarity and simplicity. You need to aim to present the person you are playing without adding any quirks or mannerisms. Let the lines speak for themselves, and do not overdo the emotions.

The big temptation will be to play the witches as cackling hags, but when you have worked on the play, you will find they are nothing of the sort. They are ordinary women who feel they possess important knowledge about medicine – about controlling life and death. They have a simple dignity as they try to hold their heads up against all the accusations flung at them.

The action is punctuated by the headlines and by Potts. The headlines are to ensure that the audience follow the rapid scene changes, and also to act as reminders of the documentary nature of the play. Potts is a kind of commentator who continually chips in with his (usually opposing) point of view.

When speaking your lines, you need to pick up cues smartly, especially Headline, Potts and the first line of each scene that comes after them. If this kind of play slows down, it quickly loses its impact.

Staging

If you are going to act the play, first make a list of all the settings. The way you arrange them must allow for very rapid transitions from scene to scene – as you must in any play written for the open stage. You need some sort of general setting in which particular scenes can be quickly identified by props or by small tables and chairs brought on by the actors. You also need positions at either side of the stage for the person who speaks the headlines. You could try an arrangement like this:

	Rostra-blocks with judges' seats	
Undergrowth curtain		Low 'cottage' doorway
Headline position	Rush matting	Potts position
Audience		Audience
	Audience	

The 'undergrowth' curtain could be strings hung with leaves which the witches and the gossips can push through. The judges' seats need to be high enough not to intrude visually until required.

For a public performance the rush matting would need to comply with fire regulations, and in any case would need to be secured so that no one can trip. Headline and Potts could sit on rostra-blocks picked out with spotlights, or up on a balcony. Potts could perhaps be writing at a desk.

The central space could have two different lighting states, a small area picked out with yellowish spotlighting to suggest candle-lit interiors, and a wider wash of light for the outdoor scenes. Lighting this play could be a useful project for a small group of technically-minded older pupils.

If you don't have stage lighting, experiment with drawing the curtains and turning on the room lighting selectively.

How to hang the witches

You need to decide whether the hangings take place off-stage or whether you try to show them.

If you choose the first, the crowd scene must be carefully orchestrated. Each gossip and each member of the crowd needs to share the same picture of what is going on, so that the scene moves uniformly towards the climax. You need to create characters through improvisation to begin with, so that the build-up isn't just mechanical but depends on believable reactions.

Groups of inventive and bloodthirsty young people may devise ways of showing the hanging on stage! One possible way would be to drop ropes (without nooses) so that they hang down behind a tall rostrum-block (perhaps the one for the judges). The witches step up from behind, with nooses of the same rope round their necks (not real slip knots). The ends of the nooses trail down loose behind the witches so that the audience may be deceived into believing they are connected to the hanging ropes. On the drum climax, the witches topple backwards on to gym mattresses, while stage hands swing the hanging ropes taut. *The whole exercise must be carried out under careful adult supervision.*

The crowd reaction is just as important in this method as in the first.

Costume

Simple seventeenth-century costume would help the play, especially long skirts for the women and tall or wide-brimmed hats and boots for the men.

Discussion, expansion and follow-up

1 Discuss your views about witches and how your views may have been changed by reading this play. Look up documentary accounts of witchcraft, e.g. Pennethorne Hughes, *Witchcraft* (Penguin); Geofffey Palmer *Witchcraft, European and African*, (Faber).

2 How far do you agree with the view that witches were the nurses and midwives of three hundred years ago, and that society could not accept that they were more successful than conventional doctors? Alternatively, how far do you agree that witches were anti-religious groups undermining morals and society in general – that they deserved all the punishment they got?

3 The play contains a lot of opportunity for movement work, ritual and improvisation. Develop your own dances and rituals and work them into a performance of the play. Use improvisation to develop the characters of the common people, and to make them more rounded.

4 Write or improvise a play which contrasts the two views of witches suggested in Number 2. Perhaps you could have two commentators, one hostile like Potts, and one sympathetic. They could call evidence in the form of dramatised scenes showing different aspects of witches' life.

5 Write a chronology (a list in date order) of the events at Pendle.

6 Write out Potts's account of his investigation.

7 Write a diary of the events at Pendle as though you were one of the witches.

8 Devise a scene between the jury members when they withdraw to consider their verdict. You could invent characters sympathetic or hostile to the witches, and don't-knows who can be persuaded. Some jury members may have cause to be thankful to the witches; others may have strong religious views.

Scapegoat

The play is set in the future on a distant planet, but it is linked to our time by the computer-recorder which Gary and Liz pick up. We are left to guess that Jana's spaceship must have come back from the future in a time-warp before burning up in the earth's atmosphere. The computer-recorder is rather like the black box flight recorder which experts recover from crashed airliners.

Jana's story, although set in the future, is similar to events which have taken place in this country in the not-so-distant past. It is about racism at one remove.

Speaking and acting the play

Liz, Gary and Jana should sound ordinary. In a different way, the computer voices should not be difficult, because in the future voice-synthesisers will be better than they are now.

The language of the councillors may be more difficult because it looks factual and unemotional. The best way to tackle it is first of all to be sure that you understand what is going on. In the first council meeting, for example, the point is that there aren't enough Zarians to work in the mines digging out the minerals which will make them rich. The second step is to decide what each councillor personally wants to get out of the meeting. In this first scene, the Employment Executive is very pleased with himself for having recognised the problem, and for having found a good solution. He's trying to put this over, and wants their agreement – and their praise. Perhaps he is a bit of a big-head.

You can look at the second council meeting in the same way. Factually, we learn that a landslide has buried all the valuable minerals. The Zarians are about to become poor again. As for the councillors, each one is trying to pass the buck – to push the responsibility on to the next one round the table.

One way you could approach this scene is to play the acting game where you sit in a circle and pass round an object which you imagine is a bomb with the fuse lit. You have to say a sentence – anything that comes into your head – before you can pass it on. When an alarm clock or timer goes, the person holding the 'bomb' is dead – out of the game – and a new round starts. Once you have got the idea of the game, you could use the dialogue of the play and build on the emotions you felt in the game.

The Speaker needs to be played by someone with the ability to phrase and pace a speech. The response of the rest of the group will be important in helping the Speaker. If available, a microphone and loudspeaker may help this scene to achieve its impact – that of a mass rally. Perhaps the crowd could have Zarian flags to wave.

The youth club members should enjoy their group spitefulness, so that Soolene will genuinely have to work hard against them. During the two halves of this scene, where do you think Jana is? Is she silent amongst the Zarians, or overhearing them from behind some corner?

You may have noticed that if Gary is changed to a girl's part, the play can easily be acted with an all-girl cast.

Staging

You have a number of decisions to make. Gary and Liz must be unobtrusively onstage all the time watching the computer-recorder. Jana must be visible as the computer-narrator, and there must be room for all the other scenes. Many of these are not precisely located, but the council meeting will need chairs and tables, and the youth club will need easy chairs or cushions. The TV studio also needs easy chairs and perhaps a 'camera'. For performance you might set up something like this:

Rally Speaker on
balcony/blocks/ladder
Council chamber

Youth club		TV studio
Liz and Gary		Jana
Audience		Audience
	Audience	

Sound effects and lighting

The computer voices should really come from a loudspeaker, and if you can fit up some form of amplification, this will help a lot. Jana's computer *could* be recorded on the cassette recorder which Liz and Gary hold, but they may lose the place, and it may not be loud enough. Perhaps the first line or two could come from the cassette and the rest from the main loudspeaker, done live.

Tape and video recording

The cross-cutting between characters makes this an interesting piece to record on tape. Can the Zarian speakers create a way of speaking that has a Zarian accent?

For video recording, you will need to find some futuristic locations (a flat roof on a modern building, for example, provided it is safe) or you might build a setting in your studio. In any case, there should be a strong contrast between the everyday realism of the scenes with Gary and Liz (the prologue and epilogue) and the Zarian scenes.

Discussion and follow-up

1 What historical occasions do you know of where leaders deliberately incited their followers to make other groups of people into scapegoats?

2 What comment does the play make on our own times?

3 Summarise the steps by which the Earthlings are turned from welcome visitors into scapegoats. Are there any clues at the outset to suggest that the relationship may turn sour?

4 How do you think it comes about that ordinary people can be turned into a mob behaving violently towards others? What steps should people take to see that this kind of thing can be avoided?

5 Write a diary of events as if you were Jana, Soolene, or a member of the Ruling Council.

6 As a group of Earthlings, compose a joint letter of protest to the Ruling Council.

7 Improvise scenes where Earthlings try to regain the friendship of ordinary Zarians.

8 Build a play, perhaps with a mixture of improvisation and writing, in which people in an imaginary society or on a planet like Zarius, step by step turn some of their number into scapegoats. At each step show how one person tips the balance against the scapegoats. (You may have heard of a playwright called Bertolt Brecht. He wrote a similar play about Hitler's rise to power, called *The Resistible Rise of Arturo Ui*. The point is, that if at each step a key person resisted, scapegoating could not happen.)